100 Fold Strength

Sterling Bristol

TABLE OF CONTENTS

INTRODUCTION

Our greatest hope, our greatest help comes from Jesus. All people need what only Jesus can give. The Word of God proves itself. I've collected one hundred of my best teachings to help people get strong. The content offers wisdom on many different subjects. These truths can relate to people from all walks of life. These articles are intentionally short and direct. This book can be used as a teaching manual or for daily meditation.

These lessons are designed to give you strength and confidence in both your spiritual and natural life. May these writings give you more revelation in how to apply God's truth for your health, happiness, and purpose in life. There is something in here for everyone. Be blessed absorbing these truths, so you can share them with others.

REAL CHRISTIANITY

Before one can understand the whole of real Christianity one must know what God's, *(Father, Son, and Holy Spirit),* plan has been for mankind since the beginning of time. Before God created Adam and Eve to start the human race, the highest form of all living creation, He planned for mankind to be with Him, to commune and fellowship with Him. He planned for mankind to be an extension of Himself throughout the earth. That's why He created mankind in His image. No other form of life had that privilege. The human race was God's treasure. He never wanted it to know sin, sickness, or death. He did not intend for humans to go to hell. That was for the devil and his evil host. So, when Adam and Eve were created they knew no sickness, sin, or death. They only knew God's goodness, peace, joy, glory and love. They were given dominion and authority over everything in the earth to rule and reign on the earth in God's glory in fellowship with Him.

Mankind lost their blessed position with God when they disobeyed God and submitted themselves to the devil when they partook of the tree of the knowledge of good and evil. Since then the earth and mankind has been cursed with sin, sickness and death. Since then no one could be good enough, or do enough of the right things to be reestablished with God being born with the sin nature. No one! So, what was God's remedy to redeem mankind back to Himself, give them eternal life with Himself, and give them the incredible blessings He originally intended mankind to live with? He sent us Jesus, and made Jesus suffer the penalty of sin, sickness and death for us, so whosoever personally makes Jesus their Lord is forgiven and made right with God again. They are given the authority Adam and Eve originally had to rule and reign on this earth in Holy Spirit power over any device of the devil.

They are born again into a new life which actually was the kind of life Adam and Eve had with God before they sinned. So, becoming a Christian is actually being reestablished with God, going back to the place God originally created mankind to be in with Him as their Father in His family. Your life becomes new because Jesus now lives in you by the Holy Spirit. You were born of the flesh. Now your spirit is born again by the Holy Spirit. You are spiritually new, reestablished to God through Jesus and headed for heaven not hell. Although God never intended people to spend eternity in hell they will unless they let the saving grace of Jesus come into their life so they can be reestablished with God. Real Christianity is personally living with God again in a super blessed life with Jesus as your Lord. Eternity is heaven guaranteed along with appropriating all the blessings God has to give you in this lifetime. Why would anyone want to resist or reject those kinds of blessings in this life and for eternity?

POSITION OF VICTORY

When a five-star general gives a command it takes him very little effort to get things done because he knows the position he is in. So it should be with every Christian. God cast Satan and his angels out of heaven down to earth. (Rev. 12:9) When God created Adam and Eve He told them to rule and reign on the earth and to subdue it. (Gen. 1:26-28) This meant God created the human race to have complete and final authority over the devil. Even though mankind lost that authority through Adam and Eve's sin, it was restored through Jesus. That means through Jesus, who destroyed the works of the devil, (1 Jn. 3:8)) we have complete authority over any sin, sickness, negativity, or oppression which the devil would try to make us live with. That's the position we were given when we gave our lives to Jesus. Any thought to the contrary is a lie from the devil.

A person can only give as much as they think they have. That's why it is so important to know how much you have received through Jesus and the total work He did for you. When you operate from the position of knowing anything of the devil is subject to you and your command in Jesus name, it securely establishes your identity as a new creature in Jesus. It takes away all the old identities to problems you thought were yours. No matter how long you identified with the labels and conditions the devil, or people, imposed on your life, one command in the name of Jesus can drive it all out of your life. That's why the Bible says we are more than conquerors. (Rom.8:37)

The world, the flesh and the devil conditions you to feeling less than who God says you are. When you identify with those lies, you have very little power to live a successful Christian life. Such was the case of the spies when they saw themselves as grasshoppers. (Num. 13:33) Problem was they were only looking at themselves and their abilities. When you look to God and His abilities you are operating from a position of complete victory and confidence regardless of the present position you may be in. Jesus totally defeated every sin, sickness, disease, injury, oppression and hurt. Why is it so hard to believe or even try to gain such victory in your own life? The battle has already been won. The victory has already been given. Take authority over those things which are contrary to your health and happiness. (Lk.10:19) You are in a position to do that at any time through Jesus. That's how God wants us to operate. He does not want suffering or hurt in our lives. Jesus paid for it all. If you have Jesus, you have victory and that victory is total!

IMAGE

When you know you are operating from a position of victory in Jesus the image you have of yourself should change. Mankind was created in the perfect image of God. (Gen.1:26) After Adam and Eve sinned, sin consciousness changed the image mankind had of itself. After Jesus paid the price for sin and forgave us, it is God's intent for us to again be changed into the image of His Son, Jesus. (Rom.8:29) This is how God wants us to see ourselves. The devil will always try to make us feel guilty and condemned for sin which has already been confessed and put under the blood of Jesus. That is just a trick to make us feel powerless and ineffective in doing God's work. That is why we must change the image of ourselves, as Christians, into the most powerful, loving people who ever walked the face of this earth. That's why the Bible states: "…let the weak say I am strong," (Joel 3:10) Just imagine how the apostle, Paul, changed the image he had of himself. After being responsible for jailing and murdering Christians, he said after his conversion, "I can do all things through Christ who strengthens me." (Phil.4:13) His thinking was changed from a sin consciousness to a Holy Spirit consciousness. This is what God requires in order to change the image you have of yourself. The sin issue has already been dealt with. The penalty for it has been dealt with. That is why the resurrected life has been given us, not the crucified life. You have got to continually see yourself in the resurrected life. The life in your human spirit is exactly that after salvation; a life resurrected over all sin, sickness and distress. When you decide you are going to live with the 'greater is He that is in you' attitude (1 Jn.4:4 kjv) the image you have of yourself will change into a security and strength you never knew. Then, in turn, you can minister the same saving, healing, delivering life and power to other people.

It is God's immense desire for people to see themselves as God has made them, i.e. in His image. If God says you can do it with His help, you can! (Phil.4:13) If God says all things are possible to them that believe, they are! (Mk.9:23) If God says no weapon formed against you shall prosper, it won't! (Isaiah. 54:17) The more you believe and act on these facts the stronger your Christian life will become. You will have a better image of yourself as you see God so actively at work in your life. His love for you has provided His character and strength which is already in your spirit in Jesus. It has been given. You have everything in your spirit which is needed to let your light shine and to overcome any dark self image the devil would still try to fool you with. It's a lie. You are forgiven and you are free. You have more strength than you can imagine because of the presence of God in your life. It is His strength which enables you to be and do everything in His image.

FREEDOM IN LOVE

When you become a Christian, your relationships with people change because your relationship with God changes. Many times a person is brought up and moves through life not knowing who they are because of other people's attitudes and expectations of them. I am specifically speaking to those who have been burdened by negative attitudes and influences put on you by family members or others close to you from childhood on up. You have lived believing if you don't do everything right and pleasing to people you will be punished or rejected. You live with a fear of rejection, so in order to feel accepted you must go beyond your own abilities, strengths and talents to please people. You live with a very defensive attitude thinking everything said around you is to be taken personally and are quick to react in order to defend yourself. There is a hidden spirit of anger on slow burn almost always at work in you ready to ignite into a big fire at the slightest of comments which would challenge your character in any way. There is a regimented feeling of perfection you must fulfill for people and no matter what you do in a legalistic way you feel it may not be good enough. This mind set is not good for you. It makes you feel like a victim in life with much fear of people.

Well, I've got good news for you! Here comes Jesus! When you let Him march into your life this is what He says, "Hi! I love you! You have never known what my kind of love is about or what it can really do for you so let's sit down and talk about it. First, I'm for real and never change, so you can trust me. That's pretty good, huh? I came to earth, took all your grief, sorrows, and struggles in life and suffered all those attitudes for you and defeated every one of them. You don't have to be burdened anymore. When I arose from the grave I left all that behind me and guess what? I gave you the same resurrected life! I gave you my resurrected self, not my crucified self. So, the day you let me into your life you crucified your poor, old, suffering, man-pleasing self and became NEW! I know you love me for giving you a brand new life with me; a life which is now filled with my love for you everyday and forever. I am more gentle and caring than any human being and have accepted you just the way you are. Now my love in your life will guide you. I am there to help protect and defend you. You are now mine. I am love. It's pretty easy not to be burdened about life and other people, now. You are now the righteousness of God in me. I've given you all the security you need in me. Just walk with me now. Release all those false responsibilities you may have felt were imposed on you. Don't take up any new ones. I have given you MY love. What you do now is in my love. You do not have to prove yourself to anyone. You are proved and approved by me. I took care of that on the cross. All I have for you is love everyday of your life. Just walk with me. Your Friend, Jesus."

WORTH

How much are you worth? You are good enough to die for. That's already happened. No debate. Thank you, Jesus. God has already shown you how much you are worth in His eyes. It is time everyone in the body of Christ realizes their total worth as a child of God. I'm not talking about seeing yourself in a prideful, haughty way. I'm talking about seeing yourself in Jesus as that pearl of great price, as that mighty warrior, as that member of the royal family, as that vessel who is so empowered by the Holy Spirit you can do all things through Christ who strengthens you. (Phil.4:13) There is no pride in that. It is simple seeing yourself as God sees you. There is no sin in feeling tremendously good every day of your life because of an activated Jesus in you. Do you see yourself like that, or are you still so absorbed in your past, your weaknesses and personal problems that you rob yourself of the vision, character, and purpose of how great the calling is on a life which is so precious to Him? If David looked to himself, he never would have defeated Goliath. If Moses looked to himself he never would have parted the Red Sea. Nobody stutters their way to stardom. There is truth to the Proverb, "For as he thinks in his heart, so is he..." (Prov.23:7)

Father God did everything He could possibly do to bring you back to Him through Jesus. We should rejoice in that fact everyday of our lives. "But he who is of a merry heart has a continual feast." (Prov.15:15) Do you want to be happy? Take pleasure in knowing Him and your worth to Him. Then you will be operating off that foundation of love, security, strength and peace which will produce fruit. The quality of the product is always related to the quality of the source. So, if you see yourself as capable of giving the very best from above, without question people will be touched with the very best and be saved, healed, encouraged! Get rid of any self-imposed image of weakness, inability, or unworthiness. The Jesus in you will move that mountain, will destroy that negativity, and will make you established in the Kingdom of God which is righteousness, and peace and joy in the Holy Spirit. (Rom.14:17) Don't believe any other thing in regards to yourself. Just seek it. (Mt.6:33) You will find it is something which is already there, and doesn't need to be given along with many other things already given to us through Jesus. When God sees how concerned we are about His things, He shows us how concerned He is about our things. Our needs are met in ways sometimes beyond our comprehension. He makes it like that, so people will know it was only Him who could do it like that. That's why He wants us to believe for the impossible, so He can do the impossible. He gets the glory. We get needs met with an enforcement of our worth to Him. The foundation we operate from is not only the Jesus who is in heaven, but also the Jesus who already resides on the inside of us. He will do the impossible in and through us because of our worth to Him.

A NEW HEART

Since the day you got saved there has been a new heart and a new spirit put in you. Everything about that newness in us leads and contributes to life; eternal life with our Savior and abundant life in this lifetime. Yet the enemy would still try to make you think what is good and of God is something which would detract from and limit our lives in some way. That's a lie. The things which detract also look good, not bad. However, the devil is always deceptive about this. It is his nature to make you think his devices lead to life even though they lead to death and separation from God. So, simply ask yourself if the things in your life help you live a strong healthy life, and contribute to increasing your relationship with Jesus. If they do you can expect God to bless your walk with Him.

Ezekiel said, "I will give you a new heart and put a new spirit within you; I will take the heart of stone out of your flesh and give you a heart of flesh. I will put My Spirit within you and cause you to walk in my statutes; and you will keep My judgments and do them. Then you shall dwell in the land that I gave to your fathers; you shall be my people, and I will be your God." (Ezek.36:26-28) Our life became new when we met Jesus. As we grow older in the Lord we must still consider it new. Every day you can expect some new thing from the Lord. It can come from the Holy Spirit or the Bible itself. It is important to remember the Gospel message is something new to the hearer. It was new when we first heard the reality of becoming a Christian. We must still present it as a new thing to the unbeliever. The world expects to hear a hum-drum religious message. That's why we must present it as something new and exciting. It is! The world looks for excitement in its' own ways. That's why we must present a God who goes beyond anything the world has to offer. God is bigger and goes farther than any imagination. Oftentimes, we have not been brought up being taught such an immense loving being. Therefore, the true God is not offered to the world. The universe is constantly expanding millions of miles a day scientists say. If that is true it would seem our God would also have to be getting bigger and bigger, being the creator of all things. All the knowledge learned about Jesus should create an excitement in the believer. This excitement should accompany the message of salvation. If it doesn't, the hearer isn't that much impressed because he/she thinks it's just a trite 'religious' message.

God is a good, loving, healing, forgiving, eternal God. This is the God each believer must carry in their heart and share. The world is the world and is accustomed to worldly ways and temporal values. They do not know of a new heart and the unchanging laws of the Spirit written on it. When we live and speak of the confidence we have in this lifetime with Jesus, our security of knowing where we will spend eternity shows forth. A strength which cannot be explained in words comes out of us. People are attracted to strong people with good values. The Lord Jesus in us speaks to people in so many different ways we can expect doors to open for us in public to share the Gospel message. It is enjoyable to live a good life. It gives us internal comfort and peace. It sets an example for others to see the changes made in us by Jesus. God wants us to thrive on the goodness provided by the Holy Spirit's activity. He wants us to live in the excitement and pleasure of His blessings. He wants us to talk about how we have been blessed, so people will know what Jesus can also do for them. He is no respecter of persons. No one is exempt from hearing the Gospel message and being blessed with all the newness and love Jesus gives.

INTIMIDATION

Take this lesson seriously and it will deliver you from any intimidation in your life. First of all, there is nothing the world, the flesh or the devil can throw at you which can intimidate you. Is this a strong statement? Yes! Why can I say that? The fact is when you respond to circumstances the wrong way you intimidate yourself; the circumstance doesn't. However, this is something you are in control of and doesn't have to happen. It's time we turned the tables on the devil and make him intimidate himself. All you have to do is show him how strong you are in Jesus! You will live without one bit of fear.

When God wanted the Israelites to enter the Promised Land they saw the giants. All except Joshua and Caleb were IN THEIR OWN SIGHT as grasshoppers. (Num.13:33) They intimidated themselves. If Joshua and Caleb didn't see themselves like that, why did they? God had already made the enemy weak in their own eyes. Rahab told the spies, "Your terror has fallen upon us, and all the inhabitants of the land faint because of you........our hearts did melt, neither did there remain any courage in any man because of you, for the Lord, your God, he is God in heaven above and in earth beneath." (Josh.2:9-11 kjv) The enemy had already intimidated himself and that included the giants!

After Nehemiah saw to it that the wall was finished after God's people returned to Jerusalem following their captivity in Babylon, their enemies, "...were very disheartened IN THEIR OWN EYES for they perceived that this work was done by our God." (Neh.6:16) Again, the enemy intimidated himself. Whenever the enemy sees God's strength he flees; and that strength is in you! So, you do not have to be intimidated by him. You make him intimidated by yourself in Jesus!

What does that mean? It means seeing yourself as a conqueror and ruler over every single thing which is evil, negative or unhealthy and living in that place. That is who God has made you in Jesus. That is who God intended Adam and Eve to be. That is the place which has already been given us in Jesus. Take it. The devil is a bunch of hot air always trying to make you believe he is a lot stronger than he really is. He is absolutely powerless against the Holy Spirit and name of Jesus. Jesus made the demons tremble. So should we. I don't care if it is a sickness, a depression, an addiction, a sin or an unhealthy attitude toward yourself or others. See it as an ant lying sideways in the grass trying to trip an elephant. You are the elephant and have the God-given mind-set of an elephant against that ant. Does God have to try hard? No! He casts out spirits with His finger! (Lk.11:20) When it comes to intimidation, the only one who can make you feel like that is yourself. Guard yourself from believing anything which would detract from the person God has made you in Jesus. That's who you are! Don't accept anything else. Just remember Joshua, Caleb and Nehemiah. Make every one of your enemies intimidate themselves as they see how strong you are in Jesus!

SUPERNATURAL LIVING

This is the norm God intended for every Christian. His intent is for divine supernatural power to be flowing through every Christian on a daily basis as needed. This is the proof of Jesus in you and the reality that Christianity is the only true 'religion'. People are attracted to the loving attitude we put forth in Christ, but that attitude was divinely received also.

First, Jesus sent out His disciples two by two and they came back rejoicing that even the devils were subject to them through His name. (Lk.10:17) They experienced the supernatural move of God through them and got results wherever they went. Then in (Mt.17:17) Jesus called them a faithless and perverse generation because they couldn't deliver the epileptic boy of his seizures. This exasperated Jesus because He knew they could have done it if they believed they could. He also confronted His disciples with their unbelief regarding the storm at sea when He said, "Where is your faith?" He expected them to calm the storm. (Lk.8:25) If we as Christians can keep all unbelief out of our lives, we will be walking, talking, anointed believers with signs and wonders following us wherever we go. We should look for opportunities on a daily basis to minister the blessings of God to people from salvation to raising the dead. Consider Moses. His faith, expressed through his action, released God to act. God is always ready to bless. He is just waiting for us to release our faith like Moses. The Red Sea was parted, but God did it through Moses. Then when water or food was needed it was there, but God did it through Moses. Paul said, "I can do all things through Christ who strengthens me." (Phil.4:13) Let your faith connect to a God who is spontaneous. (Heb.11:6) "But without faith it is impossible to please Him, for, he who comes to God must believe that He is, and that He is a rewarder of those who diligently seek him." God is a present God; not a 'was' God. "Let us therefore come boldly to the throne of grace, that we may obtain mercy and find grace to help in time of need." (Heb.4:16) Expect God to do things at your time of need. Isaiah quotes in (48:3), "I have declared the former things from the beginning; They went forth from my mouth and I caused them to hear it; Suddenly I did them, and they came to pass." You will see God do things suddenly in your own ministry as you pray in faith, without any unbelief, and continue to pray/use authority until you break through. All you need is faith without any unbelief. God and His word do not change. "Jesus Christ is the same yesterday, today and forever." (Heb.13:8) God is calling out of His body believers who will believe in a gate-crashing God and take the kingdom of God by spiritual violence if they have too. You know, it's fun seeing people saved, delivered, and the works of the devil destroyed wherever you go. Let's party!

ACCEPTED

"To the praise of the glory of His grace, by which He made us accepted in the Beloved." (Eph.1:6) You must know all of what God has done for you when you received Jesus. Otherwise you will not be able to live and minister the success God has planned for you. That's why the apostle, Paul, prayed, "that the God of our Lord Jesus Christ, the Father of glory, may give to you the spirit of wisdom and revelation in the knowledge of Him, the eyes of your understanding being enlightened; that you may know what is the hope of His calling, what are the riches of the glory of His inheritance in the saints, and what is the exceeding greatness of His power toward us who believe according to the working of His mighty power…" (:17-:19) Paul wanted their eyes to be opened so they could see what has already been done for them and who God has already made them to be in Jesus. How many requests are still made asking God to do something He has already done? How many requests are made asking God to make you into somebody you already are? The glory of God lives on the inside of every believer. Every believer has the power to cast out demons, lay hands on the sick, and see people delivered in the name of Jesus. (Mk.16:17,18) Without the understanding of the complete person God has made you to be in Jesus you will be inadequate to pray and minister these things. You have got to claim what has been already done for you; that Jesus has already won the battle you are trying to fight; take the God-given authority you have and with confidence speak the word of God through to victory. Do not doubt the power of God which is already on this inside of you ready to be released. Why does the word of God encourage us to stay filled with the Spirit? It's so the glory on the inside of us can continually be released. Knowledge without understanding can be used incorrectly. That's why the word used must be in agreement with the Spirit. As a Christian matures more of this is understood and each individual ministry produces more and more fruit. The sword of the Lord gets sharper and sharper when spoken and motivated by the Holy Spirit.

Salvation was already provided before you got saved. All you did was receive it. If that was true about your salvation, it is also true about your healing, your deliverance from certain things, your happiness, etc. All you have to do is receive those gifts also. Whatever you have received from the Lord, you have the power to release the same blessing to others because your faith in receiving it for yourself has been completed in that area. If you know that your salvation is true then you have the ability to minister salvation to others because your faith is complete in your own salvation experience. Do not think the person God put on your heart to witness to will 'someday' be in a position to hear the gospel. Jesus said, "….LIFT UP YOUR EYES AND LOOK ON THE FIELDS FOR THEY ARE ALREADY WHITE TO HARVEST." (Jn.4:35)

CONTROLLING EMOTIONS

"He who is slow to anger is better than the mighty, and he who rules his spirit than he who takes a city." (Prov.16:32) You can control your emotions. God controls His. It's not the things that happen in your life which make or break you. It's how you respond to them. You have that choice. When the Israelites made a golden calf it angered God so much He wanted to destroy everyone except Moses and his family line. Moses talked God out of it reminding God of His promises, His integrity and His Word. God changed His mind and emotions about how He was going to respond. (Exodus 32:10-14)

Consider Joseph. At first his own brothers wanted to kill him, but sold him as a slave. He became the ruler of Egypt second only to Pharoah. When his brothers came down to Egypt for food many years later Joseph could have killed them out of revenge or hatred. If he did he would have messed up God's whole plan of redemption eliminating the line of people through whom Jesus would come. Joseph chose to love them regardless of what they did, knowing God had placed him in Egypt to provide for his own. (Gen. Ch. 45)) Consider David. He could have killed Saul twice, once in the cave, (1 Sam.Ch. 24) and once at the campsite, (1 Sam.Ch. 26). Instead he showed Saul his mercy. First, he only cut off his robe; second, he only took his spear and cruse of water. He proved to Saul his respect, regardless of the fact Saul was still trying to kill David even after David spared him the first time. Consider Esau. After Jacob stole Esau's birthright and blessing, they were reconciled years later each trying to out-give each other making peace. (Gen.Ch. 33)

Consider Jesus. He could have called 12 legions (72,000) angels to help him escape the crucifixion if he chose to. (Mt. 26:53) But, He knew what he had to do, and more importantly be who He had to be, the Savior. He had to overcome all the emotions involved in going to the cross for being perfect. He did. He was righteously angry in the temple when He overturned the tables of the moneychangers. (Mt.21:12) He was sorrowful until death (Mt.26:38) as stated in the garden. He overcame all His emotions in order to succeed in His life and mission. The same Jesus lives in us with the same overcoming power! You can act like a Peter and go around cutting off ears, (Jn.18:10) or try to call fire down on anybody you feel is unrighteous, but like Jesus said, "You do not know what manner of spirit you are of." (Lk.9:54,55) We have been given the fruit of the Spirit for our emotions to line up with. When we think and feel in terms of love, joy, peace, long-suffering, gentleness, goodness, faith, meekness and temperance, we are walking in the Spirit without offense to others or self. (Gal.5:22-25) The words we speak are indicative of our emotions. If we keep our emotions right, our words will be right. We will be speaking life and edification to the hearers. This in turn will come back to you and keep you happy!

USING WHAT YOU HAVE

You have gifts and talents nobody else has. This applies to natural and spiritual things. That's why God created us as different individuals; so we can serve God and others in ways nobody else can. Often your gift will compliment the gift in someone else and together you will serve God and others. Why do you think Jesus sent out His disciples in twos? (Lk.10:1) This is one of the reasons.

You do not have to wait to receive something big before you continue to develop your natural and spiritual life. It is a matter of using what you have in order to accomplish what is ahead of you. When Samson was in a fix a jawbone was all he needed. (Judges 15:15) When Moses needed to turn the bitter waters sweet all he used was a tree. (Ex.15:25) When tax money was needed all that was needed was a fish. (Mt.17:27) When direction was needed all God needed was a speaking mule. (Nu.22:28-30) When good disciples were needed all Jesus needed were fisherman. (Mt.4:18-19) When water was needed all Moses had to do was speak to the rock. Instead he struck it. For this reason God would not let him into the Promised Land. (Nu.20:8-12) God's ways are not man's ways. God makes it like that so He gets the glory. He required Gideon to reduce the number of his army to 300, "lest Israel claim glory for itself against Me saying My own hand has saved me." (Judges 7:2) So, what you may think is a ridiculous way of being led, or strange action to take may be what God requires, so, you can only say God produced the fruit. No human effort made Jericho's walls fall. All it took was a God directed shout. (Joshua 6:20) Moses tried to add his own human effort to God's instructions and suffered because of it. Most often you don't even need any special talent, gift, or ability. All you have to do is speak the words God gives you. Throughout the book of Acts, all the disciples had to do was speak to see Jesus work through them. The same applies to us.

When Samuel was sent to choose a king from Jesse's children it was expected one of David's older brothers would be chosen. But the Lord told Samuel, "....for the Lord does not see as man sees; for man looks at the outward appearance, but the Lord looks at the heart." (1 Sam. 16:7) David was the least expected son to be chosen, but he was the one. You may think God wouldn't consider you to do something in His plans, but you are the one to do it. David was the least; Gideon was the least, the fishermen were the least, but that's who God chose. God can use anything you have to accomplish His purposes; mostly your words. Just don't be afraid to try. You will be amazed at how much God can do with a willing heart. That's where He looks. If you want to serve Him He already knows that and will open every door needed for His work to be accomplished no matter who you are.

THE WAY IS PREPARED

"For we are his workmanship, created in Christ Jesus for good works, which God prepared beforehand that we should walk in them." (Eph.2:10) The importance of this scripture cannot be overstated. When you come to the realization that God has already gone before you and prepared the way when He calls you to do something, you will walk in the boldness and confidence that will get attention. It will also give you perfect peace and security in what you are doing.

Consider what happened when Jesus entered Jerusalem for the last time. His disciples asked him where they were going to spend the Passover, (last supper). He told Peter and John to go into the city to find and follow a man carrying a pitcher of water into a house. Then he told them to ask the Master of the house "Where is the guest chamber to eat the Passover?" Then he told them the Master of the house would show them an upper room furnished and made ready. They went and it happened just like Jesus had said. (Lk.22:7-13) The way was prepared. When Jesus entered Jerusalem he sent two of his disciples into the village to find a colt tied no man had ever ridden and to loose it with the owner's permission because Jesus had need of it. They went, found the colt, and brought it back just like Jesus had told them. (Lk.19:29-35) The way was prepared. When Peter went up onto the rooftop, fell into a trance, and had a vision three times showing him not to call anything common or unclean which God had cleansed, the men from Cornelius's household were already near the city to find Peter to bring him back to Cornelius. He went with them, preached and everyone in this Gentile household got saved and filled with the Holy Spirit. (Acts Ch.10) The way was prepared. When Saul (Paul) was knocked off his horse, and struck blind he asked the Lord what he must do. The Lord said for him to go into the city and it would be told him what he must do. Jesus had showed Ananias in a vision to go to Paul, minister to him to receive his sight and be filled with the Holy Spirit. He obeyed and it happened. (Acts Ch. 9) The way was prepared.

Why do we put a question mark where God puts a period or an exclamation mark? The will of God will never take you to a place where the grace of God will not protect you, provide for you, and anoint you to do the work He calls you to. It's simply a matter of obedience to act and see your purposes from God in your life fulfilled. The above examples are only a few from scripture, but they prove God's preparation of our steps; even to the finest of details. All He calls us to do is listen and go.

So, if you already know what your calling, purpose, or ministry is continue to move toward it or deeper into it. You will find the anointing on your life is stronger than it has ever been. Now is the time God wants to do things on such a grand scale it will shock the world. But it will only happen through us as we act in faith. Don't worry about exactly how to do it. God is more concerned about faith than He is form. All He wants from us is our obedience to listen to Him. Then we act in faith according to what we hear. You will see God manifest Himself to you on a daily basis as you magnify the name of Jesus in everything you do. GO FOR IT!!!!

FEAR

"God has not given us a spirit of fear but of POWER, and of LOVE, and of a SOUND MIND." (2 Tim. 1:7) Right here fear is identified for what it is, a spirit. It is not an attitude, not an outlook, not an assumption, or any other emotional get-up. It is just a spirit as easily overcome in Jesus name as any other nuisance. "There is no fear in love, but perfect love cast out fear: because fear involves torment. But he who fears has not been made perfect in love." (1 John 4:18) You belong to God where there is no torment. Slip everyday into the security of that mind-set from the moment you wake up claiming every promise in (Psalm 23, and 91) to be yours throughout the day. You will not fear. Every time Jesus was challenged by the devil He answered with the Word and the devil left Him. (Matt.4:3-11) We do the same. Fear is based on something evil or negatively imagined which hasn't happened yet. If it hasn't happened yet who says it's going to happen? So, what right do we have, especially as Christians, to presuppose such bad things? What right do we have to imagine an evil or negative side of any situation when nothing but good and honesty is before us. It is an attempt of the devil to keep you from trying, from trusting, from going forward in doing things for yourself and Jesus. The very first words spoken by the angel of the Lord on the day Jesus was born were, "Do not be afraid: for, behold, I bring you good tidings of great joy which will be to all people." (Lk.2:10) That promise and fact is as active in every day of your life as it was on the day Jesus was born.

Let's ask ourselves if we are trusting in our own strength or the strength and wisdom of the Lord which is in us. Common sense will also keep fear out of your life and save you a lot of prayer time. The Bible says to do all things in moderation. (Phil.4:5 kjv) You will save yourself, your friends, and your creditors a lot of headaches......Did your dog really need caviar and expensive toe polish?

We are living in a time when all end time events are coming to a head. The dark will get darker, but the light will get lighter. We are the Christians the Old Testaments heroes envied, (Heb.11:39,40) knowing the glory of God which is upon and in us, walking with the glory of God shining out of each pore. Lift your spirit to the place God is pouring out His Spirit. You will see yourself triumphing over every evil, negative, thought, hurt, sickness and activity in your life and in others. The gates of hell and all its' stupid fears shall not prevail against the church of the living God (Mt.16:18) because it is so much more powerful than the defeated devil. The church has turned from the mouse it once was into a lion. Grrr.

CONFIDENCE IN PURPOSE

When God calls you to do something you need no other confirmation. The confidence in your journey is always there in the knowledge God called you to it. Joseph, at the age of seventeen, had two dreams. First, the sheaves bowing down to respect him; second, the sun, moon and eleven stars doing the same. The symbols in these dreams meant his family. He knew this was of God. (Gen.37:7,9) God's favor was on him. Even though he went through hard times, God's favor never left him. He was Potiphar's slave. "And his master saw that the Lord was with him and that the Lord made all he did to prosper in his hand." (Gen.39:3) He was in jail. "...the Lord was with him, and whatever he did, the Lord made it prosper." (:23) Finally, he was ruler over Egypt second only to Pharaoh. (Gen.41:40) This was twenty-two years later. When his brothers appeared scripture says, "Then Joseph remembered the dreams which he had dreamed about them...." (Gen.42:9) "And they bowed their heads down and prostrated themselves."(Gen.43:28) Joseph never deterred from the path he was on, hard times included, because he knew God was involved in everything he did. Job also did not stop saying the things which were right about God and got back twice as much as he lost. (Job 42:7,10) Where you go the anointing of God goes with you. When you leave the anointing should stay in the places you bring it. I believe many have an apostolic anointing and don't even know it. Jesus told Paul what his purpose was from the beginning. He knew he had to bring the gospel message to the Gentiles. (Acts 26:16-18) His rational mind was probably debating the issue, but being confronted by Jesus himself made him stick to his purpose even to the end. His anointing remained in the places he traveled. When he went to Ephesus, "...all who dwelt in Asia heard the word of the Lord Jesus, both Jews and Greeks." (Acts 19:10) The impact on what we do in Jesus name is already in God's mind before we do it. We do not have to know the outcome beforehand. I doubt we will ever know in this lifetime the impact of the seed we plant in good ground which may produce one-hundred times and more. But God does! That's why like Peter we may be called to households like that of Cornelius which was totally against the law at that time. However, the whole household got saved and filled with the Holy Spirit. (Acts 10:28, 44-48) All Peter had to know was that Jesus sent him. After Nehemiah saw to it that the wall was finished after God's people returned to Jerusalem following their captivity in Babylon, their enemies, "...were very disheartened in their own eyes for they perceived that this work was done by our God." (Neh.6:16) Again, the enemy intimidated himself. Whenever the enemy sees God's strength he flees; and that strength is in you! So, you do not have to be intimidated by him. You make him intimidated by yourself in Jesus! The true church is being called to take bigger steps. As the steps enlarge, so does the anointing on each new step. Our confidence in purpose increases as we see God working with us in obedience to the calling on our life. We are no different from Joseph, Paul, or Peter. All they needed to know was that God called them. That is all we need to know to be completely confident in everything we do in the almighty, precious, powerful, holy, anointed NAME OF JESUS!!!

CONFIDENCE—ANOINTING

After Peter and John were released from prison they got with their own company. In unity they prayed for boldness to speak the word. When this happened the place was shaken. They were filled with the Holy Spirit. They spoke with boldness. Great power and great grace came upon them. (Acts 4:23-33). This was boldness given by the Holy Spirit, not a bunch of words shouted from their brains. First they were filled with the Holy Spirit. Once that happens, you know you are speaking God's words for that moment. Your confidence has as much power in it whether you speak in a whisper or a shout. All you need to be is God inspired from the beginning. When you work on knowing God, you gain insight on how He speaks, when He speaks and what He speaks. This is for a specific purpose at a specific time. It happens through us.

On the other hand, if a person wavers, that person will not receive anything from the Lord. A double-minded person is unstable in his/her ways. (James 1:6-8) Isn't it easier to live with faith than without it? James states it is imperative that it comes from the Lord. The underlying condition is relationship. If you have confidence in the person you are with you are willing to believe and repeat what you hear from that person. Right? So it should be with God. We know God's word is true. THE ANOINTING FOLLOWS THE USE OF IT! As we use, apply, minister the word to ourselves and others that initiates God's responsibility to perform it. It is up to us to start the process. Once started, God watches over His word to perform it. He is still watching over the words He gave to the writers of all sixty-six books of the Bible. They had confidence in what they heard from God and wrote it down. Ever since then He has watched over and performed all His truth in and through anyone who has had the same confidence in God as those writers. Confidence in the word is confidence in God because God and His word are one. Our confidence is the result of knowing it works when we use it. Just be convinced that it's true and that truth works. The anointing increases as we practice it. The world practices lies. That's why it is in the shape it's in. What if all lies were replaced with all truth? The whole world and everything in it would be beautiful. Someday that's going to happen. When Jesus returns to rule and reign on this earth there will be no more war or sickness or sin of any kind. It's because truth will prevail. Jesus called Himself the truth, the only truth. There will be no more fear then. Since we have the greater power living in us there should be no ungodly fear in us now. Shout the truth at that problem if you have to. You will find our God shouting out the answer when we shout confidence over the matter. When we shout, God shouts! Just be strong!

25

AUTHORITY

If you ask Jesus to save and/or heal someone you are asking Him to come back down to earth and get whipped again and to suffer the cross again. HE HAS ALREADY DONE EVERY-THING HE COULD DO TO GET EVERYONE SAVED AND HEALED! It is our responsibility to apply what He has done. The apostles knew the responsibility they had, so let's take a look at their ministry:

THE APOSTLES' MINISTRY—They never prayed for Jesus to do it and then waited. They spoke the miracle into existence through use of His name. Of course Jesus was doing the miracle, but they acted as channels of His power and love:

(Acts 3:6) Peter said, "In the name of Jesus Christ of Nazareth rise up and walk."

(:16) "And His name through faith in His name has made this man strong."

(Acts 4:10) Peter explains, "let it be known...that by the name of Jesus Christ of Nazareth... this man stands here before you whole."

(Acts 2:43) Many wonders and signs were done through the apostles.

(Acts 4:29, 30) Apostles prayed for God to grant them freedom boldly, "by stretching out Your hand to heal and that signs and wonders may be done through the name of Your holy Servant Jesus." They acknowledged who was doing the healing (God) and that it was done by them speaking the word boldly in Jesus name.

(Acts 5:12) through the hands of the apostles many signs and wonders were done.

(:16) a multitude gathered from the surrounding cities to Jerusalem bringing sick people and those who were tormented by unclean spirits and they were all healed.

(Acts 6:8) And Stephen full of faith and power did great wonders and signs among the people.

(Acts 9:17) Ananias laying his hands on him (Paul) he said, "the Lord Jesus, who appeared to you on the road as you came has sent me that you may receive your sight and be filled with the Holy Spirit."

(Acts 22:13) Paul tells of his conversion, "Ananias...came to me and he stood and said to me, Brother Saul, receive your sight."

(Acts 9:34) Peter said, "Aeneas Jesus the Christ heals you. Arise and make your bed." Then he arose immediately.

(Acts 9:40) But Peter put them all out, and knelt down and prayed. And turning to the body he said, "Tabitha arise." And she opened her eyes, and when she saw Peter she sat up.

(Acts 14:3) Paul and Barnabas spoke boldly in the Lord, signs and wonders were done by their hands.

(:9, 10) Paul,…seeing that he had faith to be healed, said with a loud voice, "Stand up straight on your feet!" And he leaped and walked.

(Acts 15:12) Paul and Barnabas declared what miracles and wonders God had worked among the Gentiles by them.

(Acts 16:18) Paul said to the spirit, "I command you in the name of Jesus Christ to come out of her." And he came out that same hour.

(Acts 19:11,12) God worked unusual miracles by the hands of Paul so that even handkerchiefs or aprons were brought from his body to the sick and the diseases left them and the evil spirits went out of them.

(Acts 20:10 kjv) Paul fell on the dead man, said, "trouble him not for his life is in him."

(Acts 28:8) the father of Publius lay sick of a fever and dysentery. Paul went in to him and prayed, and he laid his hands on him and healed him.

NOTE: I believe in the cases where it's recorded they prayed first, e.g. (Acts 9:40, 28:8), it was a prayer asking God how He wanted them to perform the miracle, because action always followed the prayer. There are absolutely no recorded cases of the apostles praying and then waiting for God to do it without them releasing their faith in one form or another. God works, moves, loves, and gets people saved and healed THROUGH HIS PEOPLE!

HOW TO MINISTER

The conditions which apply to you as a minister are the same conditions which apply to living a normal Christian life. Whether you are ministering salvation, healing, or any other Christian activity you must be led by the Holy Spirit in what you say and do. This comes by experience in using the Word, the gifts and talents God has given you. Pray continually and ask for a daily infilling of the Holy Spirit.

It is important to be in the right place with God before you minister. All unconfessed and un-repented of sin should be confessed and repented of. That opens the door for you to be used in a limitless way by God. When your conscience is continually clear it is easy to minister with a freedom in the Spirit which allows Jesus to move in ways beyond your imagination. (Eph.3:20) Staying right with God is living a very exciting life because you are truly staying in a very personal relationship with Him. This close relationship allows you to know what to do and how to do it. Sin is bondage. Holiness is freedom. Never get those two confused with each other.

You must let your faith work by love. If you are always walking is love and a free conscience the anointing comes easy. You break through quicker in prayer and you have God's wisdom on issues. Get all unforgiveness out of your own life and admit to Jesus you can't do anything without Him. Never make a person feel guilty or condemned. Just show them your love and care for them in Jesus.

Sometimes people have to be taught first. Know the Bible good enough to teach what they need to receive. (Lk.6:17), "...they came to hear and be healed." Then minister and let the word work itself. Don't force it. The word has enough power to bring itself to fulfillment. Sometimes the greatest miracles happen in quietness.

The greatest miracle you can work is getting a person saved. That should be our priority. (Dan.12:3), "...they that turn many to righteousness shall shine as the stars forever and ever." However, Jesus said to believe Him for His works also. (Jn.14:11) So, we do His works also. How? First determine in your heart when you minister to a Christian who is sick or troubled that the problem in their body has already been totally defeated and destroyed by Jesus and that it has absolutely no right to stay in the person's body. Convince the person of that if you have the time before you pray. If the person is not saved tell them of these facts. Lead them first to the Lord if you can, then pray. Convince yourself the sickness or disease must obey when you speak because of the greater power in/through you in Jesus name. Don't ever try to fight the battle against that sickness. The battle has already been won before you pray. Convince yourself of that first. Then use the authority in Jesus name and tell it to go. Holy Spirit will give you different words for different situations, but this is the principle to ingrain in your spirit first. You will see Jesus do miracles on a continual basis and this should be daily Christian activity if needed. Most churches won't teach this because they don't have the faith to believe it but this is what the Bible teaches. First put the totally healed image of that person in your spirit before you pray, then press through until the condition of the body matches the image you have in your spirit. King David did. (1 Sam.17:46). Sometimes things beyond your control in the other person will block it—but try.

If you are praying for a person at a distance, pray as if he/she were standing right in front of you with the same principle. The Holy Spirit will often confirm when you have pressed through. Follow up with the person if manifestations don't happen instantly. Then their confidence in Jesus will increase because that is who you are representing. Live with an offensive, victorious mind-set in Jesus. Then no fear can bother you and you are carrying the anointing. There are a myriad of ways God moves and His anointing works. Be free to move with His leading. This lesson is given to help make your foundation stronger not only in ministering, but just living a Christian life. Principles are the same.

END TIME GLORY

"The glory of this latter temple shall be greater than the former." (Haggai 2:9) "…And the light of the sun will be sevenfold, As the light of seven days, In the day that the Lord binds up the bruises of His people And heals the stroke of their wound." (Isaiah 30:26) The great outpouring of the Holy Spirit all over the earth will be seven times greater than His glory in the early church. It is going to be done through His people. God is increasing His anointing toward this place. It will be manifested. He is calling His people to rise up and gain His presence at this level. Nations will be shaken through His people. "…For you are the temple of the living God. As God has said: I will dwell in them And walk among them. I will be their God; And they shall be My people." (2 Cor.6:16) The body of Christ has got to realize this is going to be done through them, not through an apathetic, misdirected, rocking chair prayer asking heaven to move without them!

If you are filled with the Holy Spirit there is power within you. There is spirit and power inherent in the word itself. There is a vast potential of power to be released from within proportionate to the amount of God's word in you. God's anointing triggers a release of the power in the word in you. "Then your light shall break forth like the morning…" (Isaiah 58:8) Paul said, "For, I consider that the sufferings of this present time are not worthy to be compared with the glory which shall be revealed in us." (Romans 8:18) "…out of His heart will flow rivers of living water…this He spoke concerning the Spirit…" (John 7:38,39) The Holy Spirit is resident within us. How much of the anointing you want is dependent on how much you want to deny your flesh and your own will. The presence of God which is already in your spirit will flow through your mind and conscience so you will know His will and Lordship in every situation. You are, "…transformed by the renewing of your mind…" (Romans 12:2) This place with Him gives you the words to speak and actions to take at any moment. We are commanded to be filled with the Spirit, (Eph.5:18) continually, (Acts 4:31) walk in the Spirit, (Gal.5:25) and pray in the Spirit. (Jude 21) When you dedicate yourself to living in His presence you move from the anointing of knowledge which is in you, (1 Jn.2:27) to an anointing for service, (Acts 2:17) to an anointing of great power. (Acts 4:33)

This walk is a walk of love with complete dependency on the Jesus in your spirit. Then the, "greater in He that is in you," (1 Jn.4:4 kjv) can come forth. The early apostles lived in the presence of the Lord. They carried the presence of the Lord with them. That's why people were healed in Peter's shadow. (Acts 5:15) That's why Stephen was so full of the power nothing could resist the Spirit in Him. (Acts 6:5,8,10) The Spirit working from the inside outwardly through words, touches, and prayers gets the job done. Our flesh is a channel for the Spirit within us to flow through. There is no limit to God's ability in and through you if your flesh is kept in subjection to the Spirit. Yes, it requires submission to the Lord at all times. The Lord is calling His people to a place where they will be used in much greater ways than the early apostles. If you are willing to pray and worship and love and act in faith like you never have done before, God will use you in that place!

END TIME CHURCH

(Hosea 6:2), "After two days He will revive us; On the third day He will raise us up; That we may live in His sight." This scripture refers to God's end-time church. In the second millennium God has revived His church. We have now entered the third millennium, (third day), and God is turning the face of His church into a bold, aggressive, advancing force which is going to shake the nations of the world. Never has the need to get ready and stay filled with the Holy Spirit been more imminent than now.

There is a new anointing breaking forth which will change whole cities, territories, and countries. It starts with us. In the past, a large part of the church has been a passive withdrawn entity. It never realized the totality of what it should be. But now, "...the manifold wisdom of God might be made known by the church to the principalities and powers in the heavenly places, according to the eternal purpose which He accomplished in Christ Jesus our Lord, in whom we have boldness and access with confidence through faith in Him." (Eph.3:10-12) This requires a bold, nonreligious, untraditional body of believers. Fresh energy and excitement will be put in these believers, so when they speak the word under this new anointing, things will happen which will get the world's attention. A greater vision and purpose to take every square inch of ground you walk on for Jesus will be manifested by these believers. They are not afraid to strike a new mark in society for Jesus. Now is the day of releasing people into this new anointing of overcoming faith and action. You can expect resistance from the traditional church world who still want to live in their lethargic, hopeless ways. Aren't those the type of people Jesus had the hardest time with? Rejoice that you know the truth. Rejoice that you know what Jesus wants to do through you in new exciting ways and act on it. Like Stephen, "they were not able to resist the wisdom and the Spirit by which He spoke." (Acts 6:10) (Hosea 6:3) "Let us know, Let us pursue the knowledge of the Lord. His going forth is established as the morning; He will come to us like the rain, Like the latter and former rain to the earth." This is the new anointing. The river of life, Holy Spirit, proceeding from the throne of God in heaven has not been totally poured out on earth. But any day God is going to push open the floodgates and the earth will be flooded just before Jesus comes for His bride. This is the day we are living in! God is searching for the people in His body who are willing to enter into and fulfill His last day purposes holding nothing back. Let's do it! First, by getting everybody in our immediate environment saved; then the city, then the state, then the country.....The anointing is here for that to happen now! GLORY!

END-TIME HOUSE

We are living in a time when the true foundation of the Lord's house is being restored to Jesus, the rock. For years, some of the 'church' has been off its' true foundation with works being built on man's ideas, and false 'religious' ideas. Now, there is attention to what Jesus is doing through the Holy Spirit. The true church is realizing it is their responsibility to act and live in faith and unity both individually and collectively. The church must fulfill all of God's end-time purposes before Jesus returns. "And that He may send Jesus Christ, who was preached to you before, whom heaven must receive until the times of restoration of all things which God has spoken by the mouth of all His holy prophets since the world began." (Acts 3:20,21) It also states it is God's intent for the church to, "....grow up in all things into Him who is the head, Christ, from whom the whole body joined and knit together by what every joint supplies, according to the effective working by which every part does its share, causes growth of the body for the edifying of itself in love." (Eph.4:15,16) Everybody in the church is important! We all are a part and have a part in bringing the whole church to its' fullness of Christ. The word tells us as His house is restored the Lord, "Will suddenly come to His temple." (Mal.3:1) When there is unity in His House, He comes quickly.

His true anointing is also being restored and increased. We should expect a divine quickening of spiritual realities and power. The prophet, Isaiah, saw this as recorded in (Romans 9:28), "For he will finish the work and cut it short in righteousness, because the Lord will make a short work upon the earth." The early apostles did not grow mature through their intellect. Jesus imparted His anointing to them through the Holy Spirit. In three and one-half years since they met Jesus, they were doing the same works He did. Jesus' goal was to replicate His ministry through them and through us. Jesus said, "I will take of mine and shall disclose it to you." (Jn.16:14 kjv) The anointing of God may be revealed to you in a different way it is revealed to others, but it is the same Spirit. The anointing on our life defines and empowers our sense of purpose on the earth. It is uniquely revealed as we are called to different functions, but all working together as stated above in (Eph. Ch. 4). His anointing can come on you in prayer, in reading the Bible, in serving others, in ministry. As you spend time with certain highly anointed people the same anointing can come on you. Elisha got a double portion from Elijah. We are coming into the fullness of Jesus being manifested in His house, the church. The early disciples were common nonreligious people. In a short period of time they were powerful apostles. What has been imparted to them has been imparted to us. As we go forth letting our Lord do a thorough and complete work in and through us, it will hasten His coming.

YOUR TESTIMONY

Evangelism is telling the truth. When you tell people how you let the truth be applied to your life, it is a witness of how Jesus can change people, giving them eternal life. The changes in your life may be different than the changes in mine. That's why there are so many different ways to tell the truth and get people saved. The apostle, Paul, stated in the first sentence of nine of his letters to the churches that he was an apostle of the Lord Jesus Christ. In his letters he told of his past; his struggles, and his new life in Jesus. He gave his testimony to convince people how Jesus changed him in his lifetime and for eternity. He said, "...how I persecuted the church of God beyond measure and tried to destroy it." (Gal. 1:13) Then at the end of this chapter he states, "And they glorified God for me." (:24)

Paul was not afraid to tell the churches of his strengths and weaknesses. Jesus was involved in both. In (Rom.7:15-25) he relates the struggles he had between his flesh and the Spirit. He said, "O wretched man that I am! Who shall deliver me from this body of death? I thank God through Jesus Christ our Lord. So, then with the mind I myself serve the law of God: but with the flesh the law of sin." (:24,25) Whether it is his or our mind, as long as we keep it hooked up to our born-again Spirit we serve God with our words, thoughts and actions. When Paul first went to Corinth he brought the testimony of God to them. (1 Cor.2:1) His testimony was the testimony of God in his life. He said, "And my speech and my preaching were not with persuasive words of human wisdom, but in demonstration of the Spirit and of power, that your faith should not be in the wisdom of men, but in the power of God." (:4,5) He was not afraid to tell them, remind them, of how God had used him when he was there, so they could also move in the power of God. Never be afraid of telling people how God is moving in your life. You are boasting in Jesus, not yourself, and giving them knowledge of how Jesus can also move in their lives. The truth cannot be denied. When the rulers, elders and scribes, "saw the boldness of Peter and John and perceived that they were uneducated and untrained men they marveled. And they realized that they had been with Jesus. And seeing the man who had been healed standing with them they could say nothing against it." (Acts 4:13,14)

Your testimony of how you got saved, how God is working in your life and using you is beyond debate or argument. It is as much proof of the need and necessity of Jesus in your life and others as the lame man at the gate beautiful who was healed through Peter and John's ministry to him. Paul said, "...woe is me if I do not preach the gospel!" (1 Cor.9:16) Like Paul, your testimony is God's testimony! It is preaching the gospel!

OUR FRUIT

Jesus said, "You will know them by their fruits," "every good tree bears good fruit." (Mt.7:16,17) When obedience to the first commandment is kept, loving God with all your heart, soul and mind, (Mt.22:37) love for people happens naturally. The world is attracted to real love. That's who God is. When our attitude of love, peace, and joy in Jesus continually flows out of us, I believe it will attract more people to the Lord than just words. In (Prov.17:17) it says, "a friend loves at all times." When you are secure in someone's love for you aren't you attracted so much the more. God's love is our love. I believe Jesus is more concerned about our attitude, than He is about our works. When we maintain a great Christian attitude, our works just happen easily because we are doing them out of an eager willingness, not out of legalistic duty. Faith works by love. (Gal.5:6) It is a tragedy that a large part of the 'church world' is still just going through the motions with a plastic smile on their face. The world observes this difference. When the early church continued in their gladness and praises to God they had favor with all the people. (Acts 2:46,47) You see, the world was attracted to their excited attitude about knowing the Lord and serving Him. The church grew quickly because of this. Jesus said in (Jn.15:11), "These things I have spoken to you that My joy may remain in you and that your joy may be full." It's the Christian's responsibility before God to bring the true meaning of love back into this world of darkness. "For God so loved....." (Jn.3:16) So many people need strength for daily living. If the joy of the Lord is our strength, (Neh.8:10) we can minister the same joy, the same strength in that joy to others every time we bring Jesus into the situation. Jesus also said in (Jn.16:22) that our joy cannot be taken from us. (Jeremiah 33:11), "the voice of joy and the voice of gladness..." We must speak with joy. We must speak with a confidence in knowing how much we are loved by God. That will influence the hearer more than just our words. As it says in the Parable of the Sower, "he that receives the seed on stony places, this is he who hears the word and immediately receives it with joy, yet he has no root in himself, but endures only for a while. For when tribulation or persecution arises because of the word, immediately he stumbles." (Mt.13:20,21) So, it really is imperative to remain happy about what you doing for the Lord. Otherwise the world will not know the difference or be attracted to what you are saying. Happiness is not something you have to work up either. Jesus has made you happy as much as He has already made you saved. No matter how much persecution Paul endured he said, "But none of these things move me; nor do I count my life dear to myself, so that I may finish my race with joy..." (Acts 20:24) He also referred to the Christians at Phillippi and at Thessalonica as his joy. (Phil.4:1) "For you are our glory and joy." (1 Thess.2:20) Happiness was and should be instantaneously generated among brothers and sisters in Christ. Everybody wants to be happy. When the world continually sees the happiness and joy that is shared by believers they will get saved because through us they will be receiving what only Jesus can give—His love!!!

BEING SUSTAINED

God is life itself. Everything which leads to natural and spiritual life is from God. The things which lead to natural and spiritual death are not. Just testing the things in your life on this basis will show you what is helping you and what is not. You know what to do about the things which are not.

Jesus called himself life. (Jn.14:6), "...and upholding all things by the word of his power." (Heb.1:3) Every breath you take is credited to our Lord sustaining you. Faith and trust in God sustaining you work together. Look at how Paul was sustained in his journeys. He was protected from stonings, from shipwreck, from snakebite, from betrayals and a myriad of other difficult situations. Look at how God sustained His people in the forty years regardless of their disobedience; manna and quail from heaven, sandals not wearing out, bitter waters turned sweet, supernatural provisions and direction by day and night. (Neh.9:21), "Forty years You sustained them in the wilderness, They lacked nothing..." As it was with the Israelites, so it is with us. Until God's purposes are fulfilled in your life, He will sustain you. Meditate on Joseph. Think about how God sustained him until His tremendously important purposes were fulfilled. The whole Hebrew race was preserved by God sustaining one man!

(Mark 11:24) presents a promise and a challenge to trust God and endure at the same time. As stated, "...whatever things you ask when you pray, believe that you receive them and you will have them." The challenge comes between the time you pray, and the time the answers to your prayers are manifested. The world, the flesh and the devil will try to stop you from believing for yourself during this time period, but God's sustaining power is always there for you to continually strengthen yourself. (Psm.94:13), "That you may give him rest from the days of adversity, until the pit is dug for the wicked." David said in (Psm. 3:5) "I lay down and slept; I awoke; for the Lord sustained me."

We have got to learn how and when to take action led by the Spirit and when to just let God be God for us. Sometimes actions are required. Sometimes we get in God's way by our actions. God knows how to protect and sustain us. He knows what we need even before we do. However, that doesn't exempt us from using common sense in life. Paul encouraged the Colossians to grow in the knowledge of God. (Col.1:10) This alone is worth more than all the granola bars and brown rice you can eat. All your cares are God's cares because you are of God. So, as the Word says in (Psm.55:22), "Cast your burden on the Lord, and He shall sustain you: He shall never permit the righteous to be moved."

LOVING ONE ANOTHER

Jesus said, "A new commandment I give to you, that you love one another as I have loved you, that you also love one another. By this all will know that you are My disciples if you have love for one another." (Jn.13:34,35) A couple chapters later in (Jn.17:26) Jesus repeats the same message when He says, "that the love with which You loved Me may be in them and I in them." Why? That the world may know. Jesus loved the world so much He died for it. There is no greater love than this. (Jn.15:13) However, if we all died for each other there would be no church left, so let's go deeper. First of all we are no longer our own. This fact has got to be realized and practiced before real selfless, unconditional love is easily given. Death to self is what allows you to love like Jesus loved. HE HAD TO DIE TO HIMSELF BEFORE HE DIED ON THE CROSS. In the garden He would not let the cup of suffering pass from Him. He said not my will but thy will be done. So, our life is a sacrifice of our own carnal will for the will of God toward each other and the world. That's why Jesus said the one who is greatest is the one who serves.

We do not have to be in any great position doing many great things to be a servant. If you make someone feel loved, appreciated and important you are being a servant. The sacrifice of a few minutes of time to say a few kind words to someone is God's love in operation. Usually it takes a very little amount of energy and resources to serve one another in meaningful ways. When your love walk with Jesus keeps growing and growing it all comes out naturally. It becomes so natural that many times you don't even realize you are doing it and are amazed at some of the things which come out of you toward people. You go home thinking, my, my, I never said or did that before but it sure worked. Sometimes you are directed by the Holy Spirit in the things you do whether or not you realize it. Then you look back and see how all the pieces fit in ways far beyond your own abilities. God will amaze you time and again when your love walk is rich. You wonder why there is so much emphasis on love. That's who God is. That is what everyone in the whole world wants and needs. The true church is the only vessel to give it. Any other worldly source has ulterior motivations and unrighteous disguises behind the so-called love it offers.

"Freely you have received, freely give." (Mt.10:8) I'm not talking about material things. It's the things God has given you to give motivated by His love. A person is more impressed by the right attitude and emotion than by the object. The love of God speaks for itself.

BODY UNITY

"But speaking the truth in love, may grow up in all things into Him, who is the head, Christ, from whom the whole body joined and knit together by what every joint supplies, according to the effectual working by which every part does its share, causes growth of the body for the edifying of itself in love." (Eph.4:15,16) There are many parts in the body of Christ. Every single one is important and helps the whole body grow. A motor is absolutely dependent on bearings as is a wheel. These are the smallest of parts, yet, without them nothing would work. With everything working there is much power and advancement. So it is with the body of Christ. The ministry of helps is as crucial as the offices. The apostle Paul listed this ministry along with apostles, prophets and teachers. (1 Cor.12:28)

In the last chapter of Romans (16:1-16) Paul salutes over thirty different individuals and households who have been helpers to him. He does this in his other letters also. Without them his trips would not have been successful. God set it up so we must depend on each other in the body. Without your brothers and sisters where would you be? As we rejoice in each other's successes and share each other's burden the spirit of unity helps and strengthens the body. This, in itself, is a witness to the world. There is so much division, competition, and confusion in a performance oriented society God does not want any of it to exist in His church. That's why He made the different parts dependent on each other with an imperative to speak and edify each other in love. Paul says, "That there should be no schism in the body, but that the members should have the same care for one another." (1 Cor.12:25) He also said to mark and avoid them who cause division and offense contrary to the doctrine you have learned. (Rom.16:16,17) Beside referring to the doctrine of serving the Lord, I'm sure he's referring to the doctrine of God's love.

The early church operated on mutual dependence. When help was needed to serve tables seven men were selected. (Acts 6:1-6) When saints in Samaria needed to be filled with the Holy Spirit Peter and John were sent. (Acts 8:14-17) The needs were the same then as they are now. God needs people to help in both natural and spiritual ways. Both share in the rewards because both contributed to making it happen. Some of the devil's favorite tools inside the church are strife, division and jealousy. If you appreciate what everybody else in doing and they appreciate what you are doing the fruit that is being produced is a result of everyone's effort. They couldn't do it without you and you couldn't do it without them so let us all rejoice together in how the Lord is using us all! The best example anyone could set in any situation is an example of love. Isn't that the example Jesus set?

EVERYDAY CHRISTIANITY

In a society where fulfillment of purpose in ever day thinking is reflected by having a great position, common responsibilities are often overlooked in the quest for that 'place' to be reached in order to initiate activity and feel appreciated. The devil uses that mind-set to make people wait to reach that 'place' before they take any action. Unfortunately they never reach that 'place'. Therefore, no meaningful action is ever taken toward purpose and people just bumble along. So it is when that worldly mind-set is transferred into Christian thinking. The word 'wait' is one of the devil's favorite words.

However, let's take a look at what the Bible says about 'wait.' (Isaiah 40:31) "But those who wait on the Lord shall renew their strength; they shall mount up with wings like eagles; They shall run and not be weary, They shall walk and not faint." The word 'wait' means serve as in being a servant. The word 'renew' means exchange. Therefore, the original meaning of this scripture could be translated; 'Those who serve the Lord will exchange their strength with God's strength then be able to run without being weary, and walk and not faint <u>WITH GOD'S STRENGTH</u>! That's exciting!

Every day in your Christian life there are opportunities to witness, serve, minister to the people and needs of those around you. You do NOT have to be in that 'place' in order to be effective and in God's perfect will. Jesus said in (Matt.23:11,12), "But he who is greatest among you shall be your servant. And whoever exalts himself will be humbled and he who humbles himself will be exalted." The Bible also says in (Gal.6:9,10), "And let us not grow weary while doing good for in due season we shall reap if we do not lose heart. Therefore as we have opportunity, let us do good to all, especially to those who are of the household of faith." You do not need a miracle ministry or be in a 'big' position in order to do the Lord's work. The widow woman will be remembered forever for her two mites. (Mark 12:42) Sometimes what you may think is the least of all personal gestures toward people will produce huge everlasting results. God knows a lot more than we do.   All you have to do is love the people around you enough to do what you can for them in both natural and spiritual ways. Your love for them will tear down the blockades which have kept them from knowing Jesus. Everyday Christianity is quite simple. It is walking in God's love, doing what you can for one another just using what you have to give. You are in a 'BIG' position with God when you live your Christian life like this. That's all you need to be concerned about. All of your goodness will be returned to you in one way or another. God makes that happen. But don't be concerned about that either. Just do what you can for people out of a labor of love because of the love God has shown you. People will get saved out of your love for them. Is there anything greater to give?

LOVING GOD

People love being loved. What about God? First think about how you respond to love. Don't you want to love, give, bless and reciprocate all the goodness you feel? God responds more than any human could, being God. God has the same needs to be loved. When you decide to dedicate your life to really loving Him, letting Him feel your love through heart-given respect and reverence for what He has done for you, important changes happen in your spiritual and natural life. Growth happens very fast for different reasons. When you live in a loving relationship with your Savior, the problems of the flesh have very little hold on you because you are walking with a conscious oneness with Jesus as He did with the Father. The work of the Holy Spirit is occupying more and more of your mind, not just your heart. Then intimacy produces trust. When you are really in love with someone you tell them more about yourself. It's the same with God. Higher levels of love—higher levels of revelation. As you love Him more and more He reveals more of Himself to you and you will continually be walking in new ways of the Spirit. God can now trust you with information because He knows you love Him enough to use it wisely.

God has always been after a love relationship with His people; not a legalistic or religious one. Love has properties nothing else has. What was once obedience out of duty, now becomes obedience out of love and joy. You want to stay right in your thoughts and actions because you have set such a high value on loving God. Obedience becomes easy. By loving God you invite His presence into your daily life and can be lifted up with automatic wisdom in any situation. Denial of self is no longer a burden. It's part of a love relationship you are enjoying; and more joy and happiness happens. You are no longer trying to win the spiritual battles by operating in the flesh. No victory is won that way. Just stop you own efforts and start loving God with all your heart and your life will be more positive than it's ever been. God accomplishes that for you. When the prodigal son returned, the Father ran to meet him, dressed him with the best robe and shoes, put a ring on his finger and had one big party. (Lk.15:20-24) It's not worth ever trying to do anything without God once you know how active His love is for you. It's more active than you realize. Loving God with all heart, soul, and mind (Mt.23:37) brings resolution to things in your natural life.

Love attracts. The early church was so in love with God and each other, they had favor with all the people and souls were added to the church daily. (Acts 2:46,47) If you are a loving individual souls will be attracted to you. So, if a church is a loving church it will get the same response from the community! Love God with all your heart and your personal life and the life of the church will work in ways beyond your imagination!

CHURCH GROWTH

First, get a vision, and keep that vision foremost in your thinking. Second, ask God what your part is if you don't know, then do your best to accomplish your part. This principle should be applied to your personal life as well. Everything must be done by faith in maintaining the realization that change happens one day at a time.

The early church started growing after everyone was filled with the Holy Spirit per the Lord's instruction. Then they walked in the Spirit. You overcome the flesh by walking in the Spirit. Don't try to overcome the flesh in order to walk in the Spirit. Commit to walking in the Spirit first, then overcoming will follow. Walking in the Word and in love keeps you. On the day of Pentecost Peter quoted Joel's prophecy, (Acts 2:16-21), then he quoted (Psalm 16:8-11) relating to the crowd what David said about Jesus:

:8 I have set the Lord always before me because he is at my right hand; I shall not be moved.
Peter preached the same security David had in the Lord.
:9 Therefore my heart is glad and my glory rejoices; My flesh also will rest in hope.
Peter preached the same happiness, the peace, the positive outlook David had.
:10 For You will not leave my soul in Sheol, Nor will You allow Your Holy One to see corruption.
Peter preached the same deliverance from hell and corruption David had.
:11 You will show me the path of life: in Your presence is fullness of joy; at Your right hand are pleasures forevermore.

Peter preached the same positive direction in life, the same joy of living in God's presence, and the same pleasures David had knowing the Lord. Peter spoke freely; (Acts 2:29) he preached the real Jesus (:36); he made an altar call (:38,39); and 3,000 souls got saved. (:41) Peter preached all these positive things and look at the response he got!

The world was so awed at the change in the apostles by the signs and wonders done in Jesus name they became afraid. (:43) Miracles will happen by walking in the Spirit. The world will know the difference in you and people will be drawn to Jesus because of it. All that believed were united in purpose and stayed together. (:44) They took care of each other and also other people. (:45) They continued daily in one accord and kept their happiness and praise to the Lord constant. What a witness! Because of this, they had favor with all the people and the Lord added souls to the church every day. (:47) I believe if we preach the same things Peter did on the day of Pentecost and follow the example of the early church we will get even more results for these are the latter days where the glory of the Lord in the latter temple will be greater and greater as we approach His coming. (Haggai 2:9)

CALLING THOSE THINGS WHICH BE NOT

God's plan from the fall of mankind in the garden has been to restore everything back to Him. Before creation there was nothing but God and everything will be in God in the end. As in (1 Corinthians 15:28), "Now when all things are made subject to Him then the Son Himself will also be subject to Him who put all things under Him, that God may be all in all." Why do you think the Bible says we are supposed to be conformed to the image of His Son now? Everybody who is not cast into the lake of burning fire will be in God. The whole process of life for eternity is restoring everything back to God through Jesus. God is a good God of perfect eternity, health, and happiness. This has been from the beginning and is the basis of our faith expectations; e.g. "calling those things which be not as though they were," (Romans 4:17 kjv), or calling into an imperfect present things of a perfect past which have been provided for us through Jesus. Right now God sees mankind perfected in Him for eternity through Jesus. Like God we must keep the end result of all our prayers and godly ambitions square in our heart and right in front of our face to overcome any negative situation in our life. This is living by faith. It is constantly telling ourself that, "What He has promised He was also able to perform." (Rom.4:21) "He who has begun a good work in you will complete it…" (Phil.1:6) That He will "give the increase," (1 Cor.3:7) and will see us through to the end results of our prayers. You can call this living by faith with the answers in our spirit and making people wonder why we smile so much when they can't see any immediate change in our circumstances. When God sees a heart with an attitude like that, he responds quickly. He enjoys our trust in Him, not ourselves.

Our walk of faith requires waiting at times while God's perfect will is accomplished. When heroes of faith are mentioned, it says out of their weakness they were made strong. (Heb.11:34) Any challenge you face in life only gives you an opportunity to get closer to and trust God more. He may teach you how to release your faith in new ways which will make your faith walk stronger. In the end you will look back and give little if any thought to the hard times of your past because of the better place God has brought you to. There is absolutely no future in your past, so don't stay there. The only things in the past you should dwell on are those blessings from Jesus you can call up into your present and be blessed, healed, set free, and made happy. Then you can say as Solomon did in (Eccles.4:15), "That which is already been, and what is to be has already been; and God requires an account of what is past." You can also require that which is past. It has been provided in Jesus. You can grow up into the blessings of God as you teach yourself not to waver at the promises and facts, and just decide you are going to receive what God says is yours in Jesus and do what God states you can do!

LIVING IN VICTORY

There is a strategy you can incorporate in your life which will keep you living in victory. That is, already knowing how you are going to respond when a weakness or temptation arises. Just think what would have happened when Satan tempted Adam and Eve in the garden and they said, "Sorry, we're not into fruit today," or when Bathsheba appeared to David he said, "I'd rather look at Mount Zion."

It is good to recognize your own weaknesses and plan how to confront them beforehand, so when they arise you will already be able to overcome. First of all, do your best to stay away from situations and people who you know will challenge your integrity as a Christian. There is enough of a challenge already just living in this world which is so much different from God's ways. When you are continually successful in overcoming, that weakness will no longer exist. (Proverbs 25:28) says, "Whoever has no rule over his own spirit is like a city broken down, without walls." It is your choice whether or not you want to overcome. The free will God gave us can be our greatest friend or our worst enemy.

Think about Jesus. He called Himself the truth. (Jn.14:6) He lived the truth. He spoke the truth. He was persecuted for the truth. He died in truth. He always knew what He was going to say beforehand, because of the time He spent with the Father. He said, "I can do nothing but what my Father has taught me." (Jn.8:28 kjv) Christians should live in the same way for Jesus said, "My sheep hear My voice and I know them and they follow Me." (Jn.10:27) Not only is this principle true in living the righteousness of God in Jesus, but it applies to doing God's work. Know how you are going to respond to an unbeliever beforehand. If you are prepared to confront lies that are believed as truth you will be very successful in soul-winning.

The whole world lives with so many lies taken as truth you must know what the truth in the word says about these situations. Jesus was the truth and He was also the word. The word will offend people and you must be willing to suffer persecution. But as people see the truth at work in your own life you are automatically providing information and evidence that your life is the truth. They will want it the more they see the truth in your life. The tighter your fellowship is with Jesus the easier the answers come. You are prepared for and able to handle every situation. Jesus knew there would be temptations, persecutions and exact timing involved in everything He did, but He was prepared to meet every challenge head on and go straight forward to the cross because of the joy that was set before Him. (Phil.2:9-11) There is great joy that is also set before us.

The more we go forth now prepared to give an answer to anyone that asks, the more joy there will be in the end. But there is always joy now in a labor of love, not one out of religious duty. Read the Bible, pray, spend time with Jesus and you will not only be preparing yourself for each situation in your own daily life, but you will also be prepared to give the right answer to others, JESUS!

GOD'S 'PERMISSIVE?' WILL

God hates sin, sickness and death. It is not part of Him. He did not create mankind with any of it. Some modern day theology talks about how God allows this or that but only to a degree before something worse happens. Wrong! God did not allow any of it. Mankind did. His grace and mercy stops mankind from seeing total disaster in many situations, but he did not allow the error or mistake leading to nearly tragic circumstances. After Adam and Eve sinned, disobeyed God and knew evil He kicked them out of the garden before they could partake of the tree of life. (Gen.3:22,23) God would not allow the knowledge of evil to exist in mankind for his eternal state of being. He would not let them touch the tree of life in the state they were now in.

God's judgment on sin is not to be confused with His divine attributes and intentions for mankind. Many times in the Bible when God's judgments fell, people died, plagues came and there was great disaster for those who were going against God and His people. The judgment of God is already on all sin and anti-Christian attitudes in this world. (Jn.3:18) That is why through Jesus a person comes out from under that judgment and into His loving grace. A Christian is now living under the blessing not the curse.

It is human nature to blame someone else for their own mistake, ignorance or carelessness. Adam did it; Aaron did it, David did it to name a few. Much of this blame-fixing is disguised when people say, "I don't know why God allowed this." He didn't allow it from the beginning, so, why should we think he is allowing it now? We allow it. Why do you think the Bible tells us to walk circumspectly, (Eph.5:15) and to renew our minds (Eph.4:23) with the word and to walk in the Holy Spirit? (Gal.5:16) It is not only for service to our Lord, but for our own protection, so we do not fall into the same traps we were once delivered out of; the same traps people in the world are still caught in. Jesus was the Word and became flesh. (Jn.1:1) We are flesh and should become the Word. Why are we called to be conformed to the image of Jesus, (Rom. 8:29) being changed from glory to glory in this lifetime? (2 Cor.3:18) It is so we can be a witness of God's GOODNESS in our life; so the world may know we are now one with God through Jesus and showing the world God's great love, joy, provision and goodness! That's who we are called to be one with in the prayer Jesus prayed in (John Chap. 17).

Every single problem in this world is due to the original sin of Adam and Eve. It is not our fault we are born with the sin nature in our flesh, but it is our fault if we respond to it and create our own problems. The Bible says to judge ourselves. (Mt.7:1-5) That's a healthy thing to do. The more you work on the strength you have in Jesus for everything, the sooner all of your weaknesses disappear. God would be contradicting Himself if He on one hand allows sin and sickness and trouble, then on the other hand gives us everything we need to destroy it. God is a good God! In eternity there will be none of it. God will be all in all in everything. (1 Cor.15:28) His perfect love will be flowing continually out of each and every heart forever. So, let's take our responsibility and walk in the light as He is in the light, (1 Jn.1:7) stay in as close fellowship with God as possible and destroy the things you may have thought God allows, first in your own life, then in whatever ministry you may have for others; this being done all through His love and goodness.

HEALING IN THE NAME OF JESUS

Let's get one point perfectly clear from the beginning: God never intended mankind to suffer sickness or disease of any kind. He saw us perfect in Him before the world was created. (Eph.1:4) He created Adam and Eve perfect in Him without sickness, sin or even death having a hold on them. They did not even know sickness, sin or death existed. All they knew were good, perfect, holy things. They and all of mankind never would have known either if they had not partaken of the tree of the knowledge of good and evil. But they did; and it was then mankind became subject to sin, sickness and death, the devil's devices. The devil wanted to get back at God. He was kicked out of heaven, so he went after the highest form of God's creation, mankind, who God created to have perfect fellowship with Himself and to have dominion over and subdue the earth. So, since the fall of Adam and Eve the devil has done everything in his power to make people sick, sinful and die and to keep them from knowing and having a true fellowship and relationship with God as Adam and Eve originally had.

Sorry devil, here comes Jesus who broke the power of sin, sickness and death in this world. He brought mankind full circle back to God with all the benefits God originally intended mankind to have. This includes perfect health. Jesus took all sin, all sickness (physical and emotional), and death upon Himself, suffered it all for you and me so we do not have to suffer. When He resurrected He gave the same resurrected power in the Holy Spirit to all who believe in Him as Savior. Any and all born-again, spirit-filled believers have the authority in Jesus and His name to destroy all physical and emotional sickness. That is a God given benefit He expects us to use for ourselves and others so we can be the happy, healthy, beautiful people God created us to be with Him. Since Jesus defeated all of the devil's work and power sickness has absolutely no right to oppress us in any way. We have been given authority over it in the name of Jesus. Let us use that authority and live perfectly healthy lives for the glory and honor of Jesus our Savior.

Jesus has the keys of death and hell. (Rev.1:18) He took them back from the devil. Then He gave the same keys to us. (Matthew 16:19), "And I will give you the keys of the kingdom of heaven, and whatever you shall bind on earth will be bound in heaven: and whatever you loose on earth will be loosed in heaven." The word 'keys' is exactly the same in both verses. It means to lock, to close. Jesus took back the power of death and everything that leads to death from the devil and He gave it to us. We, as Christians should be going around closing down and shutting up the works of the devil wherever we go! The revelation these two scriptures provide will turn you into a spiritual giant the moment you put them to use in your life.

PEACE

In a world full of war, hunger, disease, and stresses of everyday life people are looking for peace. It can only be found in and through Jesus. All other ways are temporal, empty and non-fulfilling. What does God say about peace through His word, the Bible?

God, the Father, gives peace: (Phil.4:7) "And the peace of God which surpasses all understanding will guard your hearts and minds through Christ Jesus."

God, the Son, gives peace: (Jn.14:27) "Peace I leave with you, My peace I give to you, not as the world gives do I give to you. Let not your heart be troubled, neither let it be afraid."

God, the Holy Spirit, gives peace: (Gal.5:22) "But the fruit of the Spirit is love, joy, peace..."

Peace was predicted to come through Jesus: (Isaiah 9:6,7) Jesus is called the Prince of Peace, and Isaiah said, "Of the increase of His government and peace there will be no end..."

Peace was promised: (Haggai 2:9) "The glory of this latter temple shall be greater than the former says the Lord of Hosts. And in this place I will give peace..."

Peace was published: (Isaiah 52:7) "How beautiful upon the mountains are the feet of him who bring good news, Who proclaims peace..."

The Lord reveals peace: (Jer.33:6) "Behold I will bring it health and healing; I will heal them, and will reveal to them the abundance of peace and truth."

The Lord gives peace: (Psalm 29:11) "The Lord will give strength to His people; The Lord will bless His people with peace."

The Lord establishes peace: (Isaiah 26:12) "Lord you will establish peace for us..."

Peace is the result of what Jesus did for us: (Col. 1:20) "and by Him to reconcile all things to Himself; by Him, whether things on earth, or things in heaven, having made peace through the blood of the cross."

Know Jesus, Know Peace! No Jesus, No Peace! It is very clear in knowing Jesus, you have the permanent peace of God. It is within you by the Holy Spirit and you have it for eternity. According to Isaiah it is ever increasing. Isn't God good?!!

LOVE

God is LOVE! (1 Jn.4:8)   Love is the greatest power there is. God loves us. The expression of God's love for us is Jesus. (Jn.3:16) When you feel love from God and from people you are motivated the right way. When you love people you motivate them. Love covers a multitude of sins. (1 Peter 4:8) Love prevents sin. When people feel love they are less apt to do wrong, for they do not want to violate or bruise the spirit of love which is already working on them. If you feel loved, it makes it easier for you to love. You want to share what you know is the best thing to share. If there is sin there is unrest. If there is love there is peace. Since Jesus is the total expression of God's love to us, He is the Prince of Peace.

Love is the bonding agent which establishes unity among believers. It is impossible for believers to be in one accord with the mind of the Holy Spirit unless love is permeating and saturating the fellowship. When that occurs miracles happen very quickly and very easily because believers want the miracle to happen and believe for the miracle to happen out of love and compassion for the one in need. The faith within each one is released with the power of the love. Faith works by love (Gal.5:6), so does prayer! You can't separate the two. It doesn't matter how loud you are or how wise you sound in the ears of men. (1 Cor. 2:5) What matters is how much real unconditional love and compassion you have for your brothers, sisters, and unsaved. (Parable of Good Samaritan, Lk.10:25-37)

Love is perfection; e.g. spiritual maturity. This is attained when you reach a point of having unconditional love in all things. (Mt.5:39-48) Every response in verses (:39-44) is one of unconditional love. Verse (:45) tells of God's impartial love and favor. Verses (:46,47) tell of having no reward in the partiality of loving and the expression thereof. Verse (:48), "Therefore you shall be perfect just as your Father in heaven is perfect." So, our degree of being perfect is based on our degree of unconditional love.

Love is knowledge. (2 Peter 1:5-8) Charity, God's unconditional love is at the top of the list in the chain of Christian attributes listed in verses (:5-7). All the characteristics of faith, virtue, knowledge, temperance, patience, godliness, brotherly kindness lead to charity. (:8), "For if these things are yours and abound, you will be neither barren nor unfruitful in the knowledge of our Lord Jesus Christ."

Love is power. (Eph.3:14-24) is Paul's prayer. The power that works in us is directly related to the love in us; power (:20), love (:17-19). Meditate on the role love fills in this prayer.

Love is the eternal result of Christianity. (1 Cor.13:8) This whole chapter describes how love is supposed to work between people. Without it nothing works toward any present or eternal Christian value. One day Christians will be living in a constant eternal state of love which is beyond human comprehension. Even though eternity will be timeless, not one second will go by that isn't filled totally with the love of God in Jesus in everything, everywhere! Jesus will light up the whole city of God by Himself, by the power of His love. (Rev. 21:23)

GOODNESS

"You crown the year with Your goodness, and your paths drip with abundance. They drop on the pastures of the wilderness, And the little hills rejoice on every side. The pastures are clothed with flocks; The valleys also are covered with grain; They shout for joy, they also sing." (Psm.65:11-13) God is good! People brought up under various 'religious' structures often do not know the goodness of God. They are not taught it, nor do they know how to receive it. When the real God is presented often you get 'one of those too good to be true' reactions. The disciples gave that response when Jesus appeared to them after the crucifixion. "...they still did not believe for joy." (Lk.24:41) We are brought up exposed to the ways of man and this world. All the self-ishness, greed and man-centered attitudes can make it difficult for a person to realize how much God loves them and how good God really is. That's why it is so important to present a God who can make a great positive change in one's life. This is in addition to having the answer to eternity in heaven secured. We still live in this world with its' evil devices. A new believer has got to know how much different their life can be for the better. That's why the apostle Paul continually wrote about being good and doing good for another. Some examples: (Gal.6:9,10), "And let us not grow weary while doing good for in due season we shall reap if we do not lose heart. Therefore, as we have opportunity let us do good to all especially to those who are of the household of faith." (1 Thess.5:15) "See that no one renders evil for evil to anyone, but always pursue what is good both for yourselves and for all." (:21) "Test all things, hold fast what is good." The world has got to know Christianity is as much for today as it is for eternity. The real Jesus, the real God of goodness has got to be revealed as a tremendous helper for daily living. When Peter said in (Mt.16:16), "You are the Christ, the Son of the living God," Jesus answered and told him it was by revelation from the Father he knew this. Peter knew Jesus was the anointed one, and he believed in an anointed, powerful, healing Savior. He was not afraid to say, "Silver and gold I do not have, but what I do have I give you: In the name of Jesus Christ of Nazareth rise up and walk." (Acts 3:6) Healing happened because Peter had the revelation of how good Jesus is and was not hesitant about being an extension of His goodness. Isn't that what God originally planned mankind (Adam and Eve) to be; an extension of his goodness on this earth? Faith works by love. (Gal.5:6) Love creates powerful changes in a person's life. Paul summed it up quite appropriately when he said in (2 Thess.1:11,12), "Therefore we also pray always for you, that our God would count you worthy of this calling, and fulfill all the good pleasure of His goodness, and the work of faith with power, that the name of our Lord Jesus Christ may be glorified in you, and you in him, according to the grace of our God and the Lord Jesus Christ."

HUMBLENESS

How much you want God's strength in your life is dependent on how much you want to submit to Him. When you realize how good it is to live on His strength, not your own, your desire to die to self on a daily basis will increase. Who is stronger, you or God? The place of submission is one of strength, not weakness. You cannot make yourself feel good unless you are living on pride and arrogance. It is when you are serving the Lord to the best of your ability He rewards you and gives you a satisfaction in your spirit which cannot be matched. This is the reward of submission. Because Solomon asked for wisdom instead of riches God made him the richest man in the world. (1 Kings 3:11-13) The Lord said if His people would humble themselves He would forgive their sins and heal their land. (2 Chron.7:14) If you humble yourself in the sight of the Lord He will lift you up. (James 4:10) God is acquainted with all your ways. You cannot flee from His Spirit and presence at any time. (Psm.139:3,7) When you do the least of things for your neighbor and live to be a blessing for the unsaved and your brothers and sisters in Christ, God knows about it. He will reward you. Your spirit man knows how enjoyable it is to live in the presence of God and desires to be in that place. God guarantees it to the humble. (Isaiah 57:15), "For thus says the High and Lofty One Who inhabits eternity, whose name is Holy: I dwell in the high and holy place with him who has a contrite and humble spirit, To revive the spirit of the humble, And to revive the heart of the contrite ones." Here again God is saying He gives His strength to those who are humble. What happens when you receive His strength? You become strong and dwell in the high and lofty places with Him! Jesus said, "Therefore, whoever humbles himself as this little child is the greatest in the kingdom of heaven." (Mt.18:4), "God resists the proud, But gives grace to the humble." (James 4:6) Have you ever considered God is just waiting for you to say to Him you are not able to do it yourself; that you are not able to overcome in yourself; that you can't change yourself for the better no matter how hard you try? Yes, He is waiting for everyone to say that so, He can give us His strength, His power, His love and everything else we need in this life. Why do we make such a struggle out of something so simple? Crush that wicked self-dependent human pride. It limits you. As David said, "I will lift up my eyes to the hills from whench cometh my help? My help comes from the Lord, Who made heaven and earth." (Psalm 121:1,2 kjv)

GRACE—HAPPINESS

"For by grace you have been saved through faith and that not of yourselves, it is the gift of God, not of works lest anyone should boast." (Eph.2:8,9) Grace did not stop after you got saved. You did not have to prove yourself to God in order to get saved. If you are still trying to prove yourself to God, He is not impressed. He is waiting for you to be still enough to listen to Him so you can be led by His Spirit, not your own.

Let's first stop and reflect upon what Jesus has done for you. You have eternal life with Him. His blessings are in your new life with Him now which are too numerous to begin mentioning. Aren't you extremely happy in knowing there is no longer any fear of death in your life? Isn't it exhilarating to know the spiritual vacuum you have desired to be filled all your life finally is filled in Jesus? Aren't you glad you can now think, act, respond and live differently with His peace inside you? Jesus has made you HAPPY! Now God wants the world to see your happiness. The more you let the world see your happiness the happier you become. Happiness is contagious. As the song goes, "He has made me glad." (Psalm 4:7) Your happiness will draw people to you. That is the door God has given you to tell people why you are happy—JESUS! Doesn't the Bible say they shall know you by your fruits? (Mt.7:16) Samson did great things but when his ability was gone where were his friends? People should be impressed by the person God has made you to be with much fruit. (John 15:5) The change Jesus has made inside you will attract attention and it should. It is a permanent change in your spirit, the real you who now hosts God's presence internally. Our own 'human' nature often does not allow us just to be still enough to listen to each other or God. But it is there where people will know you care when you take time to listen. As God continually exercises His grace and forbearance toward us we are showing the same grace toward others when we take enough time to find out how we can really help them. You will make anyone happy when you extend the same grace toward them as God would. It is in this place God will give you more of His wisdom. In His wisdom is every other wisdom needed to help, encourage, strengthen and minister to others. This process of giving will continually make you a stronger and more effective witness. As God's grace is unconditional so should ours be. This is the fruit the world does not understand but is attracted to. Your happiness is a product of God's unconditional love for you. The same happiness will come forth in others as we extend the same unconditional love which will lead them to salvation.

VISION

"Where there is no vision the people perish." (Prov.29:18 kjv) "Do not remember the former things, nor consider the things of old. Behold, I will do a new thing, Now it shall spring forth, Shall ye not know it? I will even make a road in the wilderness And rivers in the desert." (Isaiah 43:18,19) "For the earth will be filled with the knowledge of the glory of the Lord As the waters cover the sea." (Hab.2:14)

The prophets of the Old Testament saw the days we are now living in and entering. God is showing present day prophets the things which are coming. As stated in (Isaiah 42:9), "Behold the former things have come to pass, and new things I declare; Before they spring forth I tell you of them." God is preparing to release new things this world has never seen before. Not only will His glory be released, but the knowledge of His glory will be known. This is why the vision in the body of Christ has got to increase in knowledge and expectation of what God is now doing. Part of the "new thing" God wants to do in each of His children is to bring a great revival for the greatest manifestation of His glory in order to bring in the greatest harvest of souls.

If the body of Christ is ready to believe, "now it shall spring forth," our faith will be moving in the most powerful anointing ever experienced. This requires our attention and surrender to God and His abilities. If we look to ourselves and our own abilities we will never be able to overcome, or grow in ways of the Holy Spirit. However, if we totally submit to God at this time, God will raise us up to new levels, with knowledge we never had, with power beyond what we have known.

If you only expect God's glory to be seen in church you are very limited in your vision. You should expect God's glory to be seen at home, in shopping malls, schools, and anywhere God wants to reveal Himself. It is never to be forgotten this is going to happen through us, His chosen vessels to glorify His name anywhere and everywhere. We are the generation God has chosen to accomplish this. God is challenging each individual to think bigger than ever before, to be led in ways like never before, and do things in ways never before done. Of course, all of this is done in compliance with the Word, and it is God doing it as we respond to the promptings of the Holy Spirit. Actually, you will find out as you go forth that the greatest of things will be accomplished with the least of efforts. This is because God is moving swiftly and more powerfully behind His words which are spoken through us. Let your God given vision grow to the greatest extent possible. Then act within that vision. You will see more fruit, more miracles and more souls saved than ever before.

LISTENING

(Psm.46:10) "Be still and know that I am God...."

(John 10:2-4) "But he who enters by the door is the shepherd of the sheep. To him the door-keeper opens; and the sheep hear his voice; and he calls his own sheep by name, and leads them out. And when he brings out his own sheep, he goes before them, and the sheep follow him, for they know his voice." (Romans 10:17) "So then faith comes by hearing and hearing by the word of God."

In a society where many things are rushed up, where demands disrupt priorities, and expectations of instant results and gratifications are common, sometimes it is hard just to be still and listen. As a Christian you will find one, if not the most exciting parts of your prayer life, is hearing from God. He already knows what we have need of. (Lk.12:30) It is by listening to Him we know how to release our faith, and be led by His Spirit. Reading the Bible is hearing from God. Receiving things by the Spirit in prayer is hearing from God. Often listening to one another is hearing from God. God speaks in many different ways because we are many different people and He knows how to relate to each one of us as individuals.

Jesus calls us His friends. (Jn.15:15) He wants us to regard the Holy Spirit as our friend also. He is always talking to us and is called the Spirit of truth. (Jn.15:26) The Holy Spirit will not only direct us in what to do, but also show us how to do it. That is how personal the Holy Spirit is. Then after we act on what we hear, we see God prove Himself through our actions and our faith grows. It all started by listening to God, His Word, His Spirit. You can get direction by the word alone. You can get direction by visions, dreams and that inner voice. All of these revelations must be within the guidelines of the Word or they are not of God. Jesus said, "...the kingdom of God is within you." (Lk.17:21) Why did Jesus say, "If you abide in Me and My words abide in you, you will ask what you desire and it shall be done for you." (Jn.15:7) Sometimes you just instantly know what to say, what to do and what to pray. You are hearing from God by the word and Spirit which you have already received in your spirit.

It is so important to act on what you hear from God. If you do it constantly your faith level will grow enormously because you will see the results of putting into action what you have heard. Eventually God will go beyond doing what you even expect and your life with Jesus gets that much more exciting. If the centurion had given heed to what Paul said about getting shipwrecked if they sailed from Crete (Acts 27:10,11,21) they would not have lost the ship and its' cargo. Peter advised to be sober and vigilant (1 Peter 5:8) in order to avoid trouble. The place of staying humble, reverent, and still in the Spirit before God, gives you the advantage of listening closely and hearing everything you need to protect yourself, and be very fruitful for our Lord.

IDENTITY/DOUBLE-MINDEDNESS

When you gave your life to Jesus you became one with God. When you married your wife/husband you became one with him/her. As a Christian you are one with your brothers and sisters. The devil is always trying to make you lose your identity of who you really are as a Christian and the position He <u>has made</u> you to be in with Himself and others. God has given you the best place in life you could possibly be in. His grace offers you peace, health, happiness, and security you never had. (Jn.10:10) So when the thoughts come which try to rob you from the new identity you have in Jesus it is an attempt to divide you from God and each other. "For where envy and self-seeking exist, confusion and every evil thing are there." (James 3:16) Thoughts are evil if they try to divide you from the blessings that are already yours as a Christian. Thinking unhealthy, negative, resentful things disassociate you from who you really are. You will not receive anything from God if you think like this. (James 1:7)

Ideas on how you must improve yourself often become very frustrating because it becomes a work of the flesh. Your flesh will never be completely perfected until you make heaven, so stop trying to establish your own righteousness/goodness. You will never be satisfied. YOU HAVE BEEN MADE THE RIGHTEOUSNESS OF GOD IN CHRIST JESUS. That's who you are now! Take a new approach to overcoming. Instead of trying to 'work' your way back into God's graces, just stop and say, "Now, these thoughts are not mine! This is just the devil's way of trying to make me respond to my own flesh instead of to my spirit where Jesus thinks and speaks in and through me. I will not lose my identity of who I really am right now and who God has made me to be in this moment of time and temptation to think different. I WILL NOT! There is too much goodness in keeping my mind stayed on heavenly ways to sacrifice my peace in catering to the devil's devices which only rob me from who I really am." If you can discipline your mind to do this every time wrong thoughts come, then you are continually establishing yourself, in your own mind, the newness you have in Jesus everyday of your life. Your mind will be renewed (Eph.4:23) to the place you will only want to think and say strong, beautiful, peaceful things about yourself and others. It requires discipline, but it is the best discipline you can give yourself. All your words come from your thoughts. People know you by the words you speak. We are called to be conformed to the image of His Son, Jesus. If we let ourselves think like Jesus would, there will be no room for double-mindedness. In Jesus, everything is new. In Jesus, you will not be robbed from who you are and be turned over to the evil devices of the devil intended to hurt you and others.

Your mind is always working for or against you. God's thoughts have been ingrained in your spirit ever since the day you were saved. God's word, the Bible, will continually strengthen your thought process, which in turn will make you know yourself as a strong person in Christ every moment in time and will not think otherwise.

A PRAYER TO START EVERY DAY WITH. READ IT OUT LOUD EVERY MORNING:

Lord Jesus, in your Name I commit my mind to your spirit within me which is righteousness, joy, peace, and love. I will think in terms of love and life which in turn will render love and life and health to my entire being and to those people and situations I have life-giving and love-giving thoughts for. In the name of Jesus I come against any thought in my mind or on my mind which is not life-giving or love-giving and totally reject them from my thinking forever. I totally rebuke reject and renounce any and all spirits which would want me to think anything evil, negative, or unhealthy. Flee right now forever and never return in Jesus name. I am free. My mind is committed to happiness, joy, love and peace by all the life-giving thoughts I have. I will continue to renew my mind according to your word Lord Jesus. In your mighty name Jesus I thank you and love you for giving me the mind you want me to have.

EXPECTATIONS

"Now faith is the substance of things hoped for, the evidence of things not seen." (Heb.11:1) "...whatever things you ask when you pray, believe that you receive them and you will have them." (Mark 11:24)

In order to make your faith work and be successful in your natural and spiritual life, you must live with positive expectations in your spirit. That is living by faith. God requires this attitude for your own good. (Heb.11:6) It is for our own good to carry the answers to our prayers in our spirits before they are manifested in our lives. This gives us a positive attitude in life. It shows our Lord faith and trust in Him. He looks for this attitude in each of His children and rewards accordingly. The Bible says of the people of faith in the Old Testament, "These all died in faith, not having received the promises, but having seen them afar off, were assured of them, embraced them, and confessed that they were strangers and pilgrims on the earth." (Heb.11:13) They knew and expected to be in heaven where they now are. "But now they desire a better, that is, a heavenly country. Therefore God is not ashamed to be called their God, for he has prepared a city for them." (:16) Notice they were persuaded, embraced, and confessed the promises and got what they expected.

Not only should this attitude be applied to our eternal expectations, but also to our expectations in the natural and spiritual lives we lead. You must believe in changes for the better, advancement in your personal life and hope for your future, that God will bring to pass what He has promised. It is much easier to live by faith than live without it. Faith must be applied to every single circumstance in your life. Without it the door to hopelessness, depression, and defeat is open. When faith is applied to everything, you are living with total victory in your spirit and cannot be shaken regardless of anything negative going on around you. They way you talk indicates what you are expecting in life. Carefully think about what you are saying because blessings and cursings proceeds from the mouth (James 3:10) and someone who is double-minded will not receive anything from the Lord. (James 1:7)

Our expectations should not only be based on what we think but also on what we do. Usually you can't have one without the other in order to get results. Abraham was justified by works when he offered Isaac, his son, on the altar. (James 2:21) You must get all fear of failure, fear to act, fear of defeat completely out of your thinking. God doesn't live there. When God directs you He has already gone before you. You can be assured your prayers will be answered according to His Word, and you can live with that confidence and expectation every day of your life.

WINNING THE BATTLE

The real struggle as a Christian is not one between you and the Devil. It says in (Col.1:13), "He has delivered us from the power of darkness and conveyed us into the kingdom of the Son of His love." It says in (Rom.6:16), "Do you not know that to whom you present yourself slaves to obey, you are that one's slave whom you obey, whether of sin leading to death or of obedience leading to righteousness?"

The Devil is defeated by Jesus. (Col.2:15) There are no ifs, ands or buts. Christians do not have to submit to or defeat the devil because he has already been defeated. As Christians we have to enforce the victory which has already been given us by keeping the devil under our feet where he belongs. The devil has no power over us as long as we resist him with Holy Spirit power. The fight was between Jesus and the devil and Jesus won. The devil has no legal right to us, and we have no excuse if we are not living in victory.

Eph.4:27 "nor give no place to the Devil." We don't have to and shouldn't.

Eph.6:11-16 To fight against him means to constantly use the greater power given us without backing down until you see his influence leave you because he knows he has to. You have told and reminded him he is defeated in Jesus name.

Gen.3:15 The Devil's defeat was predicted since the beginning.

Rev.1:18 Jesus has taken the keys of death and hell and given to you the same keys to use to rule and reign on this earth. You don't have to pretend to do the job Jesus has already accomplished. You only have to stand behind the finished work with the authority given you.

2 Cor.3:17 "Where the spirit of the Lord is there is liberty."

Isaiah 59:19 "When the enemy comes in, like a flood the Spirit of the Lord will lift up a standard against him." The enemy gets flooded when he comes in. The spirit of the Lord is in us. We put him to flight.

Isaiah 10:27 "And the yoke will be destroyed because of the anointing."

Mk.5:10,12 All the demons were begging Jesus in complete submission.

Lk.10:19,20 "I give you authority to trample on serpents and scorpions and over all the power of the enemy, and nothing shall by any means hurt you." The spirits are subject unto you.

Mt.18:18 "Whatever you bind on earth will be bound in heaven, and whatever you loose on earth will be loosed in heaven."

Mt.16:18 "The gates of Hades shall not prevail against it." (i.e. the Church of the living God.)

Ok, we have got the devil's defeat established. So, the real question is how much do you let the Holy Spirit lead you? Human willpower never works. (Rom.8:13 kjv) states, "For if you live after the flesh you shall die, but if you through the Spirit do mortify the deeds of the body you shall live." That is the question and that is also the answer to living in victory. You will be tempted because of the sin condition in your flesh you are not responsible for. You were born with it and have to live with it. But temptation is not sin, so don't let the devil make you feel condemned if that happens. It is only when you submit to it that it becomes sin. You resist any temptation long enough and sooner or later that temptation will no longer exist. Neither let yourself feel condemned for sins you have already confessed and repented of. They are gone. That's also why we must forgive one another. The devil is a deceiver and would often try to make you feel guilty for sins you never committed or for sins that are gone. Never hold grudges against people who have also been forgiven. Love Jesus so much and want to stay so close to Him and His word that you can laugh at any way the defeated devil would try to con you and say, "Who do you think you are trying to kid? I'm a child of the Most High God in complete control of my flesh and will put a severe beating on you if you try to stay in my presence one second longer." Get spiritually aggressive—it works!

TAKING THE LIMIT OFF GOD

Once you are saved by accepting Jesus as Savior the process begins of letting Him become Lord in all things. You realize it's not who you are, but how much you allow the God in your spirit to rule you. You take all limits off the work and blessings of God in your life. When you put God first in all things regardless of circumstances you will not limit Him. God chose to make man's spirit His dwelling place. When you choose to let Him rule His household, which is your mind and body, he will move you into a deeper relationship with Him toward the same spiritual dimensions as Jesus had with the Father. God will lead you there step by step as you trust His word and are not afraid to test His word. Your Christian life can be based on experiences with God and the move of the Holy Spirit in your life instead of just head knowledge. As you get built up to the position of God's strength operating in your life, then you can bring revival and restoration to others. Speak, act and live with the mind-set of taking the limits off God.

<u>For your strength</u>:
(Psalm 27:1) The Lord is the strength of my life.
(Phil.4:13) I can do all things through Christ who strengthens me.
(Jerem.16:19) Oh Lord my strength and my fortress, my refuge in the day of affliction.

<u>For your needs</u>:
(Psalm 84:11) No good thing will He withhold from those who walk uprightly.
(Phil.4:19) My God shall supply all your need according to His riches in glory by Christ Jesus.
(Matt.6:33) But seek first the kingdom of God and His righteousness and all these things shall be added to you.

<u>For your confidence</u>:
(2 Tim.1:7) For God has not given us a spirit of fear but of power and of love and of a sound mind.
(Psalm 23:4) I will fear no evil for You are with me.
(2 Cor.2:14) Now thanks be to God who always leads us in triumph in Christ.

<u>For my health</u>:
(Exodus 15:26) ...I am the Lord who heals you.
(Psalm 103:1-3) Bless the Lord......who heals all your diseases.
(Exodus 23:25) I will take sickness away from the midst of you.
(Psalm 107:20) He sent His Word and healed them.
(James 5:15) And the prayer of faith will save the sick and the Lord will raise him up.
(Malachi 4:2) But to you who fear My name The sun of righteousness shall arise with healing in His wings.
(Isaiah 53:5) and by His stripes we are healed.
(Matt.8:16,17) He cast out the spirits with a word and healed all who were sick.

(Matt.4:23) And Jesus went about all Galilee teaching... preaching... healing all kinds of sickness and all kinds of disease among the people.

(Prov.4:20-23) My son, give attention to my words… for they are life to those who find them and health to all their flesh.

(1 Peter 2:24) ....by whose stripes you were healed.

God is a God of answers. His answers are in and through Jesus and the Word. When you face any kind of a problem, especially one you have not yet overcome, say I will take the limits off God in this situation! I will not limit God. I know His love for me is limitless. I will allow God to reveal Himself to me by His Spirit and know what action to take. I will not limit my faith in Him and the authority given me to release. It is from a limitless God. I allow myself to continually be made anew through my relationship with a limitless God. My God who is so good I can't stop sharing Him with others.

FAITH IS

"Now faith is the substance of things hoped for, the evidence of things not seen." (Heb.11:1) Substance and evidence are both present things. When you look at a tree do you wait for it to be a tree? When you hear a sound do you wait for it to be a sound? No! Faith is as present and real as that tree and sound. Our Lord, Jesus, acts and moves through present, immovable faith. He does not move through, "Well, I hope so, maybe, if..." type. God requires faith to give and receive. When the definition of faith is quoted, it's often misquoted without the NOW, which is the most important word in the definition. Sometimes Jesus just spoke the healing or deliverance into being. Other times, He would ask the question, "Do you believe?", before He ministered. When Jesus ministered to the woman who had a spirit of infirmity for eighteen years, first, He said, "Woman, you are loosed from your infirmity." And He laid His hands on her and immediately she was made straight and glorified God. (Lk.13:12,13) There is a very strong faith message here. First Jesus stated the impossible according to the natural mind, something He required the woman to believe and receive. Then He acted by laying hands on her and her healing happened. She had a large part to do with it even if it isn't stated. Whether we are praying, ministering, or receiving we are required to believe for the impossible with NOW faith. Don't act before this point is settled in your spirit. Jesus said, "All things are possible to him who believes." (Mk.9:23) We have a God who is so big He is beyond our comprehension. That's why it is so necessary to live by faith; big, expectant NOW faith. If it means believing for the impossible, do it. Expect God to do so much more than we can imagine. That's where He lives and that's where we should, "live and move and have our being." (Acts 17:28) All expectations should be NOW expectations, NOW miracles, NOW healings, NOW breakthroughs! Don't try to work up your faith. You will be operating in the flesh. Relax and be still in order to step from the realm of the flesh into the realm of the Spirit. All miracles in the Bible were impossible according to the natural mind. They still are. That's why it's so important to believe in an impossible God who will do impossible things NOW. Jesus was always calling those, "things which do not exist as though they did." (Rom.4:17) The same works He did we shall do and greater works. (Jn.14:12) We should be going around taking complete authority over those things which are not of God; calling into the present the blessing of God with NOW faith. You won't be making a fool out of yourself. You will be showing the world what a fool the devil was, is, and always will be. If God is a God of the impossible, you as a Christian are also a person of the impossible. In your Christian journey you will move from faith in God to operating in the faith OF God. Are you willing to think that big? That faith will shake our community, our state, our nation, and our world.

NOW FAITH

Often faith is thought of being about something happening in the future instead of the present. That's because it's been taught like that, if at all. However, the Bible states in (Heb.11:6) that, "...he who comes to God must believe that He is and that He is a rewarder of those who diligently seek Him." Also in (2 Cor.6:2) it says, "...now is the accepted time; behold, now is the day of salvation." Everything available through your salvation is available to receive and give on a daily basis. Yet, many people just live with a 'hope so' attitude. Consider the woman with the issue of blood. (Lk.Chap. 8) She was healed immediately after she fought her way through the crowd to touch Jesus. He did not even know who touched Him, so it was not a pre-planned event in His mind. Yet, virtue went out of Him when her spirit touched his Spirit. That's when her healing happened. After she identified herself Jesus told her it was her faith that healed her in that moment of time. So, what does all this mean? It means Jesus is as present today as He was then. It means as you are diligent in your faith, belief, and present trust, your spirit can touch His Spirit at anytime to receive or give things as did that woman. Never overlook the now word which is present in such scriptures as (Eph.3:20), "Now, to Him who is able to do exceeding abundantly above all that we ask or think according to the power that works in us." Works in us when? NOW!

There is no such thing in God's book as a 'defensive' prayer like, "Oh, God please don't let this or that happen or get any worse or let this situation continue, etc." You need to be delivered from that spirit of fear which is binding you up. You are supposed to charge the gates of hell in Jesus name and destroy every evil work with a totally offensive mind-set with the authority given you, NOW! Command the devil and his works to bow at the name of Jesus and leave. Jesus never prayed a defensive prayer. Neither should we. (1 Cor.2:12), "NOW we have received not the spirit of the world, but the spirit who is from God that we might know the things that have been freely given us of God." God gave us all the spiritual power we need to destroy everything which is evil, negative, and unhealthy. Yet, too often people just wait for God to intervene while they continue to live with their problems without using NOW faith.

God has timing in His program of events from Genesis to the end of Revelation. However, do not confuse that timing with receiving the things which have already been freely given us such as salvation and healing. They are available now. Reach out and grab them for yourself and minister those things to other people NOW.

Try to find where Jesus established a calendar beforehand with peoples' names on it to touch like the woman with the issue of blood or blind Bartimaeus. You won't. He healed and saved the people who came to Him in that moment of time. The same will happen in and through us. Be bold and use NOW faith and authority!

RECEIVING

Sometimes prayers do not get answered because the approach to God is wrong. First of all, the blessings of God have been given through Jesus. Yet, many believers keep asking God to give when it is actually a matter of receiving what has been given. So, the question is how do you receive? Take for example the Canaanite woman whose daughter was vexed with a devil. First she came demanding and did not even get a response from Jesus. Then she came worshiping, (Mt.15:25) got His attention and got her answer because of her faith in Him. The leper in (Mt.8:2) came worshiping and was immediately healed. The ruler whose daughter was dead also came, worshiped Jesus (Mt.9:18) and saw his daughter raised from the dead.

Everything in the world has a price on it and is obtained by how much you have to do or pay to get it. God's ways are not man's ways. His love is unconditional. Jesus said, "According to your faith let it be to you." (Mt.9:29) There are conditions in receiving blessings such as those just mentioned, but don't be a Martha and think you need to earn them. (Lk.10:38-42)

Salvation
> (Acts 10:43) "...through his name whoever believes in him <u>will receive</u> remission of sins."
> (James 1:21...) "<u>receive</u> with meekness the implanted word which is able to save your souls."

Holy Spirit
> (Acts 8:14,15,17) "Now when the apostles who were at Jerusalem heard that Samaria <u>had received</u> the word of God they sent Peter and John to them: who when they had come down prayed for them that they <u>might receive</u> the Holy Spirit... Then they laid hands on them and <u>they received </u>the Holy Spirit."
> (Acts 19:2) He (Paul) said to them, "<u>Did you receive</u> the Holy Spirit when you believed?"

Healing
> (Acts 9:17) Ananias said to Paul, "...the Lord Jesus...has sent me that you <u>may receive</u> your sight and be filled with the Holy Spirit."

Power
> (Acts 1:8) "But you <u>shall receive</u> power when the Holy Spirit has come upon you and you shall be witnesses to Me..."

Word
> (1 Thess.2:13) "For this reason we also thank God without ceasing because when <u>you received</u> the word of God which you heard from us, <u>you welcomed</u> it not as the word of men, but as it is in truth the word of God..."
> (Mark 4:20) "But these are the ones sown on good ground those who hear the word <u>accept it</u> and bring forth fruit some thirty-fold, some sixty, and some a hundred."

<u>Prayer</u>

(Mt.7:7,8) "Ask and it shall be given ...For everyone who asks,<u> receives.</u>.."

(Mt.21:22) "Whatever things you ask in prayer believing you <u>will receive.</u>"

(John 16:24) "Ask and you <u>will receive</u> that your joy may be full."

(Psalm 24:4,5) "He who has clean hands and a pure heart Who has not lifted up his soul to an idol nor sworn deceitfully—He <u>shall receive</u> blessing from the Lord and righteousness from the God of his salvation."

INCREASE

"But the path of the just is like the shining sun, That shines even brighter unto the perfect day." (Prov.4:18) As the coming of our Lord gets nearer and nearer, so does His presence and anointing here on earth on and through His people. He prepares the people who are willing to fulfill His end time purposes. Everything you have experienced as a Christian is the foundation for your next step, next level of spiritual experience and work for our Lord. Didn't David kill a lion and a bear before he killed Goliath? Wasn't Jesus, Himself, prepared for His own crucifixion by Moses and Elijah on the mount of transfiguration? (Luke 9:31) Many people want the "great" anointing without activating their faith on the level they are on.

The Lord requires growth. This requires activation. Didn't the apostle John speak to little children, young men, and fathers in the 2nd Chapter of 1st John? He was addressing believers on three different levels. As said in a previous lesson you can move from an anointing of knowledge to an anointing of service to an anointing of great power. This never comes by waiting for it. It comes by growing into the purposes God planned for you (Eph.2:10) through the use and activation of the things God has given you to do and use.

Submission to God is the one and only key that opens up all the rest of His blessings. Submission is great! It adds to your life in spiritual and natural ways. It only limits the things which are trying to rob, steal and kill you. Since Jesus came to give life, and give it more abundantly (Jn. 10:10) you are submitting to an abundant life when you submit to God. It is then He is able to do exceedingly and abundantly more than we could ask or think according to the power that works in us. (Eph.3:20)

I believe God is waiting for a people who are so sold out to Him, that the people around them can not deny who the real God is anywhere at anytime. "For everyone to whom much is given, from him much will be required…" (Luke 12:48) The rewards of any personal sacrifice for His glory is so much greater than any temporary inconvenience the flesh may have to endure. So what? The flesh is going to die anyway, but that which is done for the Lord will last through eternity. Remember the widow with only two mites? (Mk.12:42-44)

The time we are living in is a time that will produce the greatest manifestation of God's glory that has ever been known. If we are willing to decrease enough so He can increase (Jn.3:30) to levels in our life we have never known, then the glory of the Lord will cover the earth.

So don't worry about what you are going to do for the Lord tomorrow. Just be faithful to the calling of God on your life on a daily basis. Take the opportunities to minister or serve on a daily basis then in time you will see how God has grown you up into new places with bigger doors with more revelation through your faithfulness. If you are faithful in little things you will grow up into bigger things. (Lk.16:10) That's how God works with you. It is wise to know what to expect in what is ahead, but never let that vision interfere with your daily opportunities because those are the things which will get you there. Amen.

WORDS

Life and death proceeds out of your mouth. (James 3:10 kjv) God created everything with His words. (Gen.1:3,6,9,11,14,20,24,26) Jesus is the Word (Jn.1:1) and the Truth. (Jn.14:6) Lies are words. The Devil told Eve a lie. She believed it, and became a liar because she believed a lie. She told Adam a lie and was cursed because the Devil is the father of lies. (Jn.8:44) See what happens when you believe and repeat a lie. You are cursed and so are the people you talk to. You are usually popular or unpopular because of the words you speak. You pronounce blessings or curses because of the words you speak. Either you are putting angels to go to work on your behalf (Psm.103:20) or you are initiating demonic activity. Let's get real. Gossip started in the Garden of Eden because people wanted knowledge. Look what getting that knowledge did. Ouch!

If someone makes a mistake how do you know whether or not they have already confessed and repented of it? They probably have; so what right does anyone have talking about something which no longer exists in God's mind. Would you like people talking about the things you did which are already dead and buried by the blood of Jesus?

The Devil loves it when you respond to wanting knowledge you shouldn't have. That's how original sin happened and that's why we all are born under that curse of original sin. The Devil's tricks are still the same. He wants us to stir up strife, and division by talking. If someone is not walking right with God pray for them, encourage them and love them anyway and keep your thoughts and words to yourself. (James 5:20) You don't pull anyone out of the fire by talking about them. Keep it personal and show love.

When people talk about other people it's an issue of pride. Under their breath they say, "See, I'm so much better than that person because I wouldn't do that and I want the whole world to know it." You are in big trouble with God and with people when you act like that because they see your pride coming out in your words. Even though some of your accomplishments are very good, it is not good to even talk about them unless you are giving God the glory for it all. Who gave you those abilities anyway?

Being humble before God it not a weak place. (James 4:10) IT IS A VERY STRONG PLACE TO BE. Don't be proud. The more of God is having the more of His wisdom, His love, His power, His anointing, His grace, His mercy and His understanding. When we esteem each other better than ourselves (Phil. 2:3) we will be offering all these heavenly resources to people and it will be done through our words. If you want to be blessed, be a blessing. God will show you how and He will put His words in your mouth.

Don't let your ears accept negativity about yourself or about anyone else. What does the Lord's Prayer say? "Be it on earth as it is in heaven..." There is no negativity, blame, accusations, or rumors in heaven. If you want to honor God in your life speak well about people and remember He is the judge, not you. Always remember how much Jesus has done for you and let the same love you have for Him be extended to other people. Your words and deeds accomplish this.

NEW vs OLD

A person living in this world of darkness long enough may find it hard to realize how new they really are once they are saved. But once this newness is acknowledged and accepted their life changes. When Paul wrote to Philemon, the slave-owner of Onesimus, requesting freedom for this slave, he said, "That the sharing of your faith may become effective by the acknowledgment of every good thing which is in you in Christ Jesus." (Philemon :6) This is almost parallel to saying your faith works by love. (Gal.5:6) There is a reservoir of love inside each one of us so far beyond our comprehension I don't think it will be totally realized until we reach heaven. Not only was Paul applying this truth to Philemon, but to the church in his house, therefore all Christians. Paul was really saying to Philemon in paraphrase, "If you could only realize what a tremendously good loving brother you are in Jesus, you would not keep Onesimus as a slave, but as a brother in Christ." There is so much goodness in Jesus that as we absorb ourselves in His being, the Holy Spirit will instantly give us the right response and reaction to every situation. Paul also reminds us that it must be done voluntarily, not out of compulsion. (:14) So herein lie the keys to receiving love for yourself. When you respond to others in love, you are going to be loved. It's the same give and it shall be given principle which applies to everything.

You must acknowledge you can draw everything from that new person you are in Jesus. That's when the 'every good thing' in (:6) must rise from your spirit at any time it needs to. It's there in every situation if you want to find it. Here, and in many other places Paul wrote about knowing Jesus. It was his desire above all things to know Jesus. (Phil. 3:8-10) This knowing is the acknowledging of what you already have and can draw from. The newness always resides on the inside of you. You don't have to ask for it. You just have to develop it into all parts of your life. You will see as you decrease your sensitivity to everything in the natural world around you and responses and reactions to it how much of the new Jesus just jumps out of you, sometimes to your own amazement. Paul wanted so much to know Jesus so he could show Jesus!!! Everywhere he went he showed Jesus. The nature of the flesh is stubborn and does not give up easy, nor does it roll over and play dead. But when we see the reward and fruit of knowing and showing Jesus everywhere we go like Paul did, it's worth keeping the old man in the grave. If you want to raise someone from the dead, just make sure it's someone who has already died physically.

MORE MERCIFUL

Often when someone teaches you about the man coming to his friend's house asking for bread in the middle of the night, and the widow who came to the unjust judge asking to be avenged of her adversary the usual slant in the explanation goes something like this: Because they were so persistent they got what they wanted. WRONG! If this was the case their reward would be determined by their own works. God is not the homeowner, neither is He the unjust judge. HE IS MUCH MORE MERCIFUL THAN EITHER OF THEM AND DOESN'T REQUIRE WHAT THEY DID:

(Lk. 11:5-8) "And he said to them, Which of you shall have a friend and go to him at midnight and say to him, Friend, lend me three loaves, for a friend of mine has come to me on his journey, and I have nothing to set before him, and he will answer from within and say, Do not trouble me; the door is now shut and my children are with me in bed. I cannot rise and give to you? I say to you, though he will not rise and give to him because he is his friend, yet because of his persistence, he will rise and give him as much as he needs." (:13) "If you then being evil know how to give good gifts to your children, how much MORE will your heavenly Father give the Holy Spirit to those who ask Him!" Jesus said just ask Him and you will receive it, seek and you will find it, knock and it will be opened. God is much more merciful than that homeowner.

(Lk.18:2-5) "There was in a certain city a judge who did not fear God, nor regard man. Now there was a widow in that city; and she came to him saying, Get justice for me from my adversary. And he would not for awhile; but afterward he said within himself, Though I do not fear God, nor regard man, yet because this widow troubles me I will avenge her, lest by her continual coming she weary me." (:8) "I tell you that He will avenge them speedily......" God is not like the unjust judge. He moves fast!

"But I will sing of Your power; Yes, I will sing aloud of your mercy in the morning; For You have been my defense And refuge in the day of trouble." (Psm.59:16) Claim them for yourself every day. "He is ever merciful and lends and His descendants are blessed." (Psm.37:26) Sometime we still think the harder we push and pull at our faith the more may get done. It won't. God is not impressed because He is seeing you depending on yourself. So, be still for some extended moments and relax yourself in God's presence. In that stillness you will develop your relationship and communication with your Lord. You will gain more wisdom in how to do things, than in all the striving you were up to. Jesus is the Prince of Peace. The peace you have accompanies you and proves you and Jesus are doing it together!

GOD PREPARES THE WAY

Before God created mankind, Adam and Eve, He created a beautiful place for them to live, the garden of Eden. When God called Abraham (Gen.12:2,3) He prepared the future several thousand years ahead of him, so, "in you, all the families of the earth shall be blessed," Jew and Gentile together in Jesus. When the Israelites left Egypt God prepared a pillar of a cloud to lead them by day, and a pillar of fire to lead them by night. (Ex.13:21,22) God sent an angel before them to keep them and to bring them to the place He had prepared. (Ex.23:20,23) God even said in (:27) He would make their enemies afraid of them before they got there. This was proven by Rahab (Joshua 2:9-11) when she said to the spies before they entered the land, "...the terror of you is fallen on us and that all the inhabitants of the land are fainthearted because of you....our hearts melted, neither did there remain any more courage in anyone because of you..." Even the enemies knew God had given the Israelites the land before they got there. How easy it would have been if only they hadn't submitted to fear. (Num.13:31-33) Before the walls of Jericho came down the Lord told Joshua, "I have given Jericho into your hand." (Josh.6:2) The Lord told Ananias what was prepared for Paul before he ministered to Paul. (Acts 9:15,16) Before Jesus left the earth He told His disciples, "I go to prepare a place for you." (Jn.14:2)

There is a calling on every Christian life. Our Lord has already ordered our steps and prepared the way for each and every one of us. He has already gone before us. (Eph.2:10), "For we are His workmanship, created in Christ Jesus for good works, which God prepared beforehand that we should walk in them." So why should there be any fear or hesitation in going forward and doing God's work knowing He has already prepared the way for us? Isn't it obvious how much we can trust God to accomplish what He calls us to? Jesus is the Alpha and Omega, (Rev. 1-11). He knows the beginning from the end and the end from the beginning and knows how to make everything work in between those two points. That's why it says in (Prov.3:5-7), "Trust in the Lord with all your heart, and lean not on your own understanding. In all your ways acknowledge Him and He shall direct your paths. Do not be wise in your own eyes....." No matter what God calls you to do, as long as you know it's from God keep doing it. God loves to prove Himself through a faithful heart. It does not matter how long it takes to get results. God will do it. "By your patience possess your souls." (Lk.21:19) When our Lord calls you to His work, don't even consider yourself in any way. Our faith is totally in Him and His abilities to perform His deeds as we just act in faith. In these end times the hearts are already ready to receive the Gospel message, and the blessings we will minister in Jesus name. God has already gone before us and prepared the way! The time is now to expect God to do things through us like never before!

OUR RESPONSIBILITY

"For the eyes of the Lord run to and fro throughout the whole earth, to show Himself strong on behalf of those whose heart is loyal to him." (2 Chron.16:9) The church world must recognize it is their responsibility to get the world saved and do the works of God. The only limitation God has is you and me. The tremendous things talked about concerning what God is going to do in the end times are going to be accomplished through you and me as believers. We all must adjust our mind-set to that fact.

When the talking is done, the praying starts. The praying continues until direction from above is given. When direction is received, actions of faith are taken. Fruit is produced. Faith is built because you see the fruit, the results of your actions. Then God will give you bigger direction, bigger purposes and on and on. None of it happens unless it's initiated by that word from God which propels you. That is not received without serious consecration before God and prayer. That's why it is of extreme importance to maintain that intimate relationship with our Lord who loved you so much He died for you. Being saved puts you into that new positional relationship, but just like in close human relationships, without that personal, daily one-on-one communication, the relationship is dry. God is so eager to do so much. He is just looking for that willing vessel to respond to His call.

God is calling everyone to do something. The people in your own personal environment are there for you to reach. That's why you are in that situation. Some people will say if I don't do it, God will choose someone else. That's just an excuse. You are called to plant the seed, i.e. give the word of God to people. The Bible says, "And how shall they hear without a preacher?" (Rom.10:14) Everyone has the ability to tell the truth. The only requirement is knowing the truth. If you know the truth, you can tell the truth. Evangelism is that simple; just telling the truth. The truth is seed. The Holy Spirit gives the increase and growth. So, by just planting the seed you are one-hundred percent successful in what you are doing. Maybe God will use a Christian television program, another Christian or just divine inspiration to bring that soul into the kingdom. You did your job by planting the seed and starting the process.

Call this just a straight inspiration message of gumption and desire to serve God if you want to. I can tell you straight out that whatsoever you do in faith in this day and age we're living in God will honor it. He will go beyond what you think He will do because of the tremendous outpouring which is happening now. If you don't try you won't see anything. If you don't give up you will be successful in everything you do. Let God show Himself strong through you and me. This is the proof which will bring people into the kingdom.

HOW QUICK?

When our prayers don't seem to get answered in the time we want them answered, our faith is tested. However, let me remind you about God's timing, especially concerning the end times we are living in. (Isaiah 65:24) states, "It shall come to pass That before they call, I will answer, and while they are still speaking, I will hear." This is nothing new with God. When Abraham sent Eliazar, his highest servant, to Mesopotamia to find a bride for Isaac, Eliazar laid down a fleece. As he approached the well to get water for himself and his camels he said, "Now let it be that the young woman to whom I say, Please let down your pitcher that I may drink and she says, Drink and I will also give your camels a drink, let her be the one You have appointed for Your servant Isaac." (Gen.24:14) (:15) states, "And it happened before he had finished speaking, that behold, Rebekah .... came out with her pitcher...." She fulfilled the conditions of the fleece before Eliazar could finish saying it.

(Amos 9:13) states, "Behold the days come, says the Lord, When the plowman shall overtake the reaper, And the treader of grapes him who sows seed..." What this means is you can expect an answer even before you ask a question. Saves you a lot of prayer time doesn't it? This realm of knowledge is having the mind of Christ.

As the days grow nearer to our Lord's return, the quicker you can expect God's purposes being fulfilled in your life. It says in (Deut.28:1,2), "Now it shall come to pass if you diligently obey the voice of the Lord, your God, to observe carefully all His commandments, which I command you today, that the Lord your God will set you high above all the nations of the earth. And all these blessings shall come upon you and overtake you, because you obey the voice of the Lord your God." Whatever overtakes you is always before you. Therefore if you are living in obedience, you are constantly moving into God's blessings, not waiting for them to catch up to you. Your Father knows your every need. He will meet every single one of them as you seek Him and His kingdom. (Lk.12:30,31) These scriptures in (Deut. and Luke) speak for themselves. It's not an automatic free ride. But if you consider the immensity of what Jesus has done for you, why wouldn't you want to do the best for yourself; and really get to know the one who saved you?

I believe the moment you pray God hears you. Again, when Daniel prayed for his people in (Dan. Ch. 9) it says while he was speaking Gabriel came, touched him and told him the meaning of the vision. (:20-27) One of the most famous faith scriptures says, "...whatever things you ask when you pray, believe that you receive them and you will have them." (Mk.11:24) If you don't get an instant answer it doesn't mean God hasn't heard you. He has and the answer is "in the works." When the devil tries to discourage you because the manifestations to your prayers hasn't happened yet, just tell yourself and the devil—IT'S IN THE WORKS AND I'M NOT GOING TO BUDGE FROM MY TRUST IN GOD AND HIS WORD. Expect it to happen quickly.

HOW GOOD?

How good is God? He is better than the human mind can imagine Him to be. When something seems too good to be true, it is often rejected with unbelief. The devil's influence on the human mind over the centuries has made one think living below par is the normal way to live, even though God intends to give you so much more. Jesus could do very few miracles in Nazareth because of their unbelief. (Mt.13:58) They could not believe Jesus could do something that good for them. When Jesus appeared to His disciples after His resurrection from the dead they could not believe it for joy. (Lk.24:41) Even though Jesus told them it was going to happen over the three years of His ministry, they still had doubts even though He stood face to face with them.

The same problem exists in the mind of people who do not go to church. They don't think God is really that good and could have a personal interest in them. It is the church's job to give the general public the right impression about how good God really is; and how much He cares about them as an individual. God will treat them a lot better than the way the world has treated them. God's ways are all good, but they are not man's ways. If you can adjust your life to doing things God's way according to the Word your life will change into something very good. Even people in some churches do not have the full realization of God's goodness and live without the expectations of receiving all the blessings God has for them. That's what 'religion' will do to you. God's love is unconditional. That's a very big word to receive in your mind; but it is true. It is also the reason you can tell people Jesus accepts them just like they are. Many will say I'm not good enough for God to love me. Tell them to let God love them through Jesus and see what happens. Any amount of self-proclaimed unworthiness to receive Jesus is a denial of God's unconditional love for them. It is just an excuse. Even after salvation, when someone may slip, God's unconditional love is always there to forgive and restore fellowship with Him.

Religious people will resist the Holy Spirit today as they did against Stephen. (Acts 7:51) However, all the works of the Holy Spirit are good! On Mar's hill when Paul spoke of the resurrection from the dead through Jesus he was mocked. (Acts 17:32) However, this is the greatest blessing any person could receive. It determines one's eternity and is what the whole of Christianity is based on.

The human mind doesn't accept or understand the impossible. All Christian promises and blessings are believed and received by faith. People need to be hopeful and expectant in as big a way as possible for God's blessings in their life. Get rid of all human evaluation. You will restrict yourself. Every time you pray and minister remember (Eph.3:20), "Now to Him who is able to do exceedingly abundantly above all that we ask or think according to the power that works in us."

THE BLOOD OF JESUS

When a patient gets admitted to a hospital, everything the doctors want to know is found through an examination of the patient's blood. So it is with Jesus. If you understand what the blood of Jesus means, you will really know Jesus and what His blood has done for you.

Let's start with (Rom.3:24,25), "Being justified freely by his grace through the redemption that is in Christ Jesus. Whom God set forth as a propitiation by His blood, through faith, to demonstrate His righteousness because in His forbearance God had passed over the sins that were previously committed." This means the blood of Jesus has made us right with God without any cost to us. That's a pretty good feeling isn't it? You are right with God. His blood has given us the right to enter into the heavenlies at any time to approach God with our praises and prayers. That wasn't possible before the veil was rent in two at the time of the crucifixion.

In the human condition we are still living in, i.e., in our flesh, our conscience will either limit or liberate us. The blood of Jesus has given you a clear conscience. (Heb.9:14), "How much more shall the blood of Christ who through the eternal Spirit offered Himself without spot to God, cleanse your conscience from dead works to serve the living God." You have been delivered from a legalistic mind-set of your own good works saving you. You no longer have to entertain any thoughts of guilt or condemnation for sins committed before salvation, or those committed after salvation which have been confessed and repented of. God does not remember them, and He does not want you to remember them either. The devil is the accuser. God isn't. Your conscience has been made right through the blood of Jesus. Just keep all sin under the blood and you can act with boldness as a true ambassador from heaven at any time. Your mind can work for or against you. That's why Jesus gave you his mind where your thoughts flow freely and you speak freely without any internal resistance. When you know your mind is right with God, your speech carries the anointing. When Jesus spoke, it happened. When you speak, the same anointing on Jesus comes through you. That's why the apostle Paul says in (Phil.2:5), "Let this mind be in you which was also in Christ Jesus." Let's face it, there is always a battle between the flesh and the Spirit, but nothing becomes sin unless you submit to it. If that happens just confess it, and your conscience is as pure as if it never happened. Don't live with hangover guilt. It will limit you and doesn't belong. The blood of Jesus conquers. (Rev.12:11), "And they overcame him by the blood of the Lamb, and by the word of their testimony....." The blood has a direct control on your words which conquer evil, sickness, and pain of any kind. As we dedicate ourselves to live with a clear conscience, our relationship with God and people will become very rich and anointed. YOU WILL WALK LIKE JESUS WALKED AND DESTROY THE WORKS OF THE ENEMY WHEREVER YOU GO!!!

VICTORIOUS LIVING

I ask you how you are doing. You say, "Oh, I'm well so far..." What? What's with the 'so far'? If you are well now, why shouldn't you be well a minute, an hour, a day, a month or a year from now? Did you just get finished watching the Wizard of Oz and expect another house to fall on you or what? You speak from fear which doesn't belong there if those words come out.

God is a God of completion. When Jesus said, "It is finished," it was finished! (Jn.19:30) Your salvation and all the blessings of God in Jesus were yours on that day and the day you received them when you became born again. They still are. Jesus died unto sin once, e.g once and for all! Likewise reckon yourself to be dead to sin once and for all. It shall no longer have dominion over you. (Rom.6:10- 14) You have been given total victory in Jesus!

When Nahum predicted the fall of Nineveh, he said, "...he will make an utter end of it, affliction will not rise up a second time." (Nahum 1:9) This is the way you should treat every single sickness and affliction which you have overcome in Jesus. Maybe you received a blessing through the faith of another person. If symptoms try to return God wants you to use your own faith to reject those symptoms, knowing Jesus and you are completely finished with it. Just tell it in Jesus name it cannot return a second time.

You ask, "Could my life really be that good?" Absolutely! When Jesus taught His disciples how to pray he told them it was His will for them to live their life on earth as it would be in heaven. That's a big statement. God's end-time people will be walking in so much love and power the tongue of every skeptic will be stilled. No one will be able to doubt God's goodness for you. Do you dare to believe in such a blessed life for yourself? I hope so. Things may be happening right now you don't even know about which will bring you to that place; a place of tremendous blessing and service to our King! The blessed promises of, "breaking the yoke from off of us and bursting thy bonds in sunder," (Nahum 1:13 kjv) are as real for us now as they were then. God wants you to personally expect all this goodness for yourself. (Isaiah 10:27) says the same thing. "It shall come to pass in that day, that his burden will be taken away from your shoulder and his yoke from your neck, and the yoke will be destroyed because of the anointing oil."

So far, have I changed your 'so far' to, "Yes, I'm doing well, and expect the greatest days of my life are right in front of me. I expect the greatest move of God in my life; beyond what I could even imagine! I know I am loved by God more than I can imagine. My expectations will come to pass and I will say as the Psalmist in (Psm.130:5,6), "I wait for the Lord, my soul waits, and in His word do I hope. My soul waits for the Lord, more than those who watch for the morning Yes, more than those who watch for the morning." EXPECT!!!EXPECT!!!EXPECT!!!

LOVE AND ANOINTING

God is love. (1 Jn. 4:8) In the beginning all that existed was God. (Gen. 1:1) Therefore, in the beginning all that existed was love. Quite a revelation when you think about it. In the end all that exists will be in God, therefore in love. So, the whole process of life, creation, downfall, and restoration from the beginning to end goes from love to darkness and evil back to love and light. Why do you think the Bible says, "faith works by love"? (Gal.5:6) Why do you think the Bible says, "For God so loved the world…"? (Jn.3:16) Why did Jesus command us to love one another? (Jn.15:17) It's because love is what makes everything work. The whole process of life is regaining and restoring love back to its' totality. That's how it's going to be for eternity. That's why Jesus taught His disciples to pray for everything on earth to be like it is in heaven.

Many times people try to make the things of God work without real unconditional love and wonder why the anointing isn't there. Without that ingredient you are without God. If you have a hard time loving people, you have a hard time loving God. First realize God needs our love. When we love God just because we want to, God rewards us with his love. It's the same give and it shall be given principle. When you know you are loved don't you want to return the same?

Since his downfall, it's easy to see why the devil has done his best to make people think God is something other than love. It's because without love there is division. Where there is division there is every evil work. Even ministry can become a dead bunch of works without love. There is no way you can work up an anointing. Just start loving, praising, worshiping God with all your heart. When that happens God returns His love. That's when the anointing comes because it's linked to God's love. Anointing and love cannot be separated. If someone is walking in the anointing, that person is walking in love. It is easy to distinguish the people walking in, living in, speaking in the Spirit of God. The love of God is enhanced through everything they do. The more a person determines to walk in love, regardless of the sacrifices required to do it, the greater the anointing will be. The presence of God will continually overshadow them. I'm sure the people healed in Peter's shadow were touched by God's love coming from him.

The world does not understand Christian love. When the glory of God is manifested they have no words to explain it because they have never felt it before. So, as usual, when God's true church gets its' heart set on showing love, the world is going to know it, want it and have it like we do. I believe the more God feels our love for Him, the more He wants to give. Aren't we like that; another example of being created in His image?

A STRONG HEART

"Therefore, be patient brethren until the coming of the Lord. See how the farmer waits for the precious fruit of the earth waiting patiently for it until it receives the early and latter rain. You also be patient. Establish your hearts for the coming of the Lord is at hand." (James 5:7,8)

What does it mean to 'Establish your heart'? It means to strengthen your hope. You know in your heart it is a given Jesus is coming back, that heaven will be your home and we will live in blessedness for eternity. God has given us that assuredness in His Word. The same strengths He has given us in our eternal outlook are the same strengths He has given us to live our lives in Him now. The same faith and expectations we have for our eternal future can be applied with the same spiritual energy for everyday living and accomplishments; be it for our needs or His. The world, the flesh and the devil will always try to make adverse circumstances seem greater than resolutions. However, you must always remind yourself that God is always greater, that you can do all things through Christ who strengthens you, that you are on the winning side with Jesus, that things will be resolved and accomplished. It's called faith at work. Our trust in God is all wrapped up in faith. By faith alone you must believe. Sometimes God is just waiting for your options to run out. When they do, that's when you allow God to go to bat for you and smack a few homers. God's ways are not man's ways. He makes it like that so He alone gets the glory. Man's ways are limited; God's ways aren't. That's why living by faith will reward you beyond what you may imagine. In yourself you will strive to fight the battle; in Him the battle is already won. In yourself you will waste time trying to figure things out. In Him it's already figured out. He knows the end from the beginning.

When your expectations seem delayed just remember the tremendous hope the farmer has. He has patience until he receives the early and latter rain. Then he gets his blessings so fast he can't keep up with them. Like it says in (Amos 9:13), "...the plowman shall overtake the reaper..." Also, in (Deut.28:1,2 kjv) it says the blessings will not only come upon you but overtake you if you hearken unto the voice of the Lord and obey His commandments. This implies being led by the Spirit and the word. God does not want His people to live with one bit of discouragement in their lives. He has already made our hearts strong in Him. All you have to do is be convinced of that. All you have to do is say I'm going to accomplish this or that because if Jesus wasn't defeated neither am I. My trust is in the one who created the whole universe. Therefore I have more than enough strength to go on and see my needs met and His kingdom established around me because it's already established in my heart!

WHAT DOES IT TAKE?

What does it take to win a soul to Jesus? In the days of the early church resurrection from the dead through Jesus was a new issue everyone was excited about. They rushed to get saved. They knew it was through Jesus they were saved. They were anxious to get their eternal life secured. In today's world heaven is not really a new issue, but the means to get there are about as scattered as bird-shot. Some people assume because God is a good God they will make heaven. Some think they lived a good enough life to make it. Some think there is no hell, so everyone goes to heaven. All wrong! In third world countries millions of people are getting saved. The reason is Jesus is their only hope. They have none of life's comforts or amenities. The fact is whether a person is rich or poor, lonely or popular, sick or healthy; there is no eternal hope for anyone except that which is found in Jesus. (1 Cor. 15:19) Just ask the thief on the cross next to Jesus. All it took was a few words.

So, what does it take to convince someone the only way is through Jesus? It is the goodness of God which leads someone to repentance. Every unsaved person lives with a certain amount of guilt. Living with guilt produces internal torment. Fifty percent of psychiatric patients are hospitalized for that reason. The good news is through Jesus every person can be set free from all internal torment besides having heaven guaranteed. In today's world there is much fear. But, perfect love casts out all fear. (1 Jn. 4:18) Also, the guilt issue is taken care of because who the Son sets free is free indeed. (Jn. 8:36) Many times people are more concerned about current issues in their life being resolved, than eternal issues. However, Jesus is the answer for both. When a person loses their own life, they will find it (Lk.17:33) not only in Jesus for eternity, but in Jesus throughout their lifetime. Salvation is the treasure of treasures in one's life. Sadly, a large part of the general population looks at it as entering something negative and binding instead of something genuinely positive, healthy and satisfying. The church's job is to present it as the grandest gift one could ever receive; a gift which not only settles one's life for eternity, but clears every bit of a person's conscience from guilt and shame. "And that you put on the new man which was created according to God in true righteousness and holiness." (Eph.4:24)

Many people haven't ever been exposed to real unconditional love. However, God doesn't have any hidden gimmicks. It's all been free for the taking every since the cross. God wants the very best for everyone in this lifetime and the next. Sometimes the unconditional love issue is contended with due to false doctrines and a person's hard experiences in life. A life with Jesus is different. It's all good! A bit of heaven is pulled down into a life with more love, strength and security than they have ever had. This is the Jesus the real church has and gives. This is what it takes!

GLORIFYING THE FATHER

While we are still living in this world, there are many things which can challenge your attitude from being positive and secure in the Lord. The world tries to program you to fear terrorism, the flu, and any effort to succeed and go on in life. There are those who will say frogs go moo, that Canadian geese fly east and west, and that chickens quack when they lay big eggs. There are those who say God only chooses some people to be saved and a rash of other errors. However, in (Gal.1:9) it says the person is cursed who preaches any other Gospel but the truth. Life in the world will produce trials of sorts, some more difficult than others; but in every situation Jesus is saying look to me! I will help you. I will give you the strength you need to overcome and be strong. The Lord is glorified in our strengths and successes, not in our weaknesses and failures. "The righteous shall flourish like a palm tree: He shall grow like a cedar in Lebanon. Those who are planted in the house of the Lord shall flourish in the courts of our God. They shall still bear fruit in old age; they shall be fresh and flourishing; to declare that the Lord is upright, He is my rock, and there is no unrighteousness in Him." (Psm.92:12-15) Your success is a witness of the Lordship of Jesus in your life. God delights in the prosperity of His servants. (Psm.35:27)

It is God's will for us to be totally dependent on Him, so He can be glorified in all we do. That's why in (Prov.3:5) it say, "Trust in the Lord with all your heart, and lean not on your own understanding." Further reading in this chapter states it will lead to health and wealth. There is no faith involved in leaning on your own understanding. God looks on our faith in Him, nothing else. God's ways are not man's ways. That's why it is exciting living by faith with expectations no amount of human reasoning or ambition can equal or produce. Jesus loves it when you cast all your cares on Him (1 Pet.5:7) because He cares for you. All provision is included in His care. "The Lord is near to those who have a broken heart and saves such as have a contrite spirit. Many are the afflictions of the righteous but the Lord delivers him out of them all." (Psm.34:18,19) When you give it all to Jesus, you lose nothing but gain everything! All your fears are gone when you seek the Lord. (Psm. 34:4)

God promises a blessed life to all believers who abide in the vine. The Father is glorified in this! (Jn.15:8) As we adjust our attitude in relating to God as our closest friend, our best helper, our trusted guardian, our immediate companion in everything, our intimacy with Him increases. He wants and needs to be glorified. He is intimate with us. He has been chasing His bride for years. He wants us to feel His love daily and respond to Him and others in the same Spirit. Our needs will be met and our attitude in life will reflect His glory in everything we do. Our strength, success, happiness, health, peace, and love show forth His glory in us!

ACTIVATED FAITH

How many times have you heard about an elderly, malnourished, run-down person who dies in a little shack not fit for a cockroach, but had a million bucks stuffed in the mattress? What good did the money do for that person or anyone else? So it is with believers who know the word, proclaim to have faith, but never use either. Everyone wants to be more 'spiritual' but that never happens without the experience of using what God has given you to use. "But strong meat belongs to them that are of full age, those, who by reason of use have their senses exercised to discern between good and evil." (Heb.5:14 kjv) This scripture talks about spiritual senses, not the five natural senses. So, plainly put, your spiritual person only grows by doing spiritual things, spiritual ways. That's why we are so encouraged to walk in the spirit. (Gal.5:16) You know the scripture, "Not by might, nor by power, but by my Spirit says the Lord of hosts." (Zech.4:6)

Our faith expectations should be larger than they have ever been. If we believe God is going to do greater things than ever before, we must be willing to take greater steps, greater faith 'chances', greater witnessing, greater praying than ever before. It doesn't happen without us. But when it does happen through us people take notice and the kingdom of God increases in our community. Let not anyone live alone with their faith. "… faith by itself, if it does not have works is dead." (James 2:17)

Works come from your relationship with the Lord, not a legalistic mind-set. When your relationship with the Lord gets bigger, your works get bigger. Don't strive to do huge things with huge expectations until your relationship with the Lord can support it. Before you do anything spend time in reverence and awe before the Lord. That invites His presence more than having a Martha mentality. The more you reverence the Lord first in all your activities, the more His presence permeates His calling on your life. Don't make resolutions for the New Year. Your flesh will make you fail. All you have to do is obey the two greatest commandments and those things on your heart will be resolved. Determine in your heart your relationship with Jesus is going to be bigger and richer than it's ever been. It is then the fruit just drips off you naturally and works follow as easy as a cat chasing a string.

This is the greatest hour on God's timetable we are living in. His glory will be upon all believers. The majority of miracles will be happening outside the four walls of the church as we carry the Good News with us wherever we go. It is time to take back what the enemy has stolen as we speak God's word to all our and others' circumstances. As it has been said about the fields, "They are already white for harvest." (Jn.4:35)

REVELATION OF JESUS

When Jesus was born angels brought the coming of Jesus and His purpose to the shepherds. The glory of the Lord surrounded them. They were convinced what the angels said was true and went to Bethlehem because of what the Lord had made known to them. (Lk.2:15) The angels were the agents to bring the good news, then they got the revelation from the Lord, Himself. I can't overemphasize the importance of this scripture. In this day and age we, as Christians, are the agents to bring the good news. After the good news is given, there will come a time when Jesus will reveal Himself to the hearer in ways which cannot be denied. The Bible calls it sealed with the Holy Spirit. Once someone is sealed their life is never the same.

When Jesus encountered the women at the well, (John Ch. 4), she received the revelation of who Jesus is, then went into the city and told the men. They came out to meet Jesus. Then it's recorded many of the Samaritans believed on him for the saying of the women who testified that Jesus told her all that she ever did. Then many more believed because of his own word; and said unto the woman, "Now we believe, not because of what you said, for we ourselves have heard Him and we know that this is indeed the Christ, the Savior of the world." (Jn. 4:42) First, many believed because of her testimony, then many believed because Jesus revealed Himself to them. Your own testimony is very important. It will draw people to Jesus. Then by the work of the Holy Spirit, Jesus will reveal Himself to the believer which will keep them believing for the rest of their life. When you share your testimony you are sharing the revelation of Jesus. This can be as new and exciting to the hearer as it was to you when you first believed.

At the time of Jesus the Good News was a new thing. Today it is not a new thing, but something which has been glazed over with layer after layer of false religious copies, ideas and idols. So, what is going to convince the hearer today? It is your confidence and boldness in what you believe. When people see how strong the Jesus is in your life you will be giving them the revelation of Jesus. This is the revelation of happiness, peace, love and power coming out of you. Why were people healed in Peter's shadow? It was because of what was coming out of him. Words are the most important thing which can come out of you. They are spirit and life. When we speak spirit and life as a habit to people and situations, that initiates the wonderful love and power of Jesus to move. Sometimes He moves in ways beyond our imagination. We bring the revelation, not just the knowledge of Jesus to a hurting lost and dying world. Just let Jesus be Himself in and through you. You will be giving out the same revelation God gave to the shepherds. It changed the world then; it will change the world now!

PRAYER AND MINISTRY

Once I was asked to minister to a woman who was terminally ill with a condition I had never ministered to. The doctors had given up. I went home that night and prayed to the Lord, "I do not know what to do or how to minister to this patient. Please show me." Immediately the Lord showed me two scriptures I had never used before; but knew they were for this lady. I ministered these two scriptures to this lady the next day and she was instantly healed. The point is, I ministered the results of my prayer and got results. Why? It was the right word of God, from God, for that moment.

(Acts 9:40) Peter knelt down, prayed, said, "Tabitha, arise." She opened her eyes, saw Paul and sat up. (Acts 28:8) The father of Publius lay sick of a fever and dysentery. Paul entered and prayed, laid hands on him and healed him. In both cases Peter and Paul got before God first to get direction in how to minister. In one case the Lord said just speak; in the other case the Lord said lay hands on. Peter and Paul ministered the results of their prayers and acted on the direction God gave them. That's why listening is such an important part of your prayer life. It gives you the anointing to get the same results as Peter and Paul.

There are the scriptures, the overall word of God from Genesis to Revelation which is referred to as the 'logos' in the Greek. Then there is that special word of God taken from the 'logos' which is revealed to you as the life-giving, anointed word for that moment which is called the 'Rhema.' This word or action is what you minister. Peter and Paul knew all the healing scriptures but acted only on what they received from God for that moment. They were led by the Holy Spirit; not just the word. They were filled daily with the Holy Spirit so they knew what to minister after they prayed. Prayer and ministry are closely related, but two different things. As a Christian learns how to listen, see, and receive the things from God in prayer, then minister those specific things, sometimes in very specific ways, that person will see God move through them consistently.

When Paul describes the armor or God in (Eph.6:13-18) he says, "having girded your waist` with truth." The truth is the word, the 'logos', the belt around our loins, the seed from our loins. (:14) Then he describes, "the sword of the Spirit, which is the word of God." (:17) This is the 'Rhema'. The sword hangs on the belt and is drawn to do battle, to conquer. So, the anointed word of God is drawn from the belt of truth with signs following. Like it says in (Mk.16:20), ".....the Lord working with them and confirming the word with accompanying signs." Sometimes people try to minister with the belt instead of the sword. Jesus didn't. When the devil tempted him in (Lk.Ch.4) Jesus answered with specific words. The devil left him. Then in (:14) it says, "Then Jesus returned in the power of the Spirit to Galilee." He was a Rhema minister. "...as he is so are we in this world." (1 Jn.4:17)

THE PRODIGAL SON

When the prodigal son returned to the Father, the Father was overjoyed and ran to meet him. This is how God responds to one of His children who return to Him. (Lk.15:20) God is calling His children to respond the same way one to another. All of us slip or have a 'bad' day from time to time. Yet, we return to God, repent, are forgiven and go on. Therefore, if a fellow Christian tries to judge or talk evil of that person they are committing the greater sin! Jesus specifically said in His sermon on the mount do not judge or you will be judged. (Mt.7:1-5) He called those people hypocrites, the same term He used regarding the Pharisees. When the lost son was wasting his life, the conviction of the Holy Spirit was on him and caused him to return to the Father. It is the Lord who chastises and disciplines His children because He loves them. (Heb.13:6,7) Yet, some people in the church would try to play God in this area. If so, they are walking in pure carnality and will be judged. The apostle Paul said, "For you are yet carnal for whereas there is among you envying, and strife and divisions are you not carnal and walk as men?" (1 Cor.3:3) He also said in (Rom.16:17), "Now I urge you brethren note those who cause divisions and offenses contrary to the doctrine which you have learned and avoid them." Whoever walks and talks contrary to love and forgiveness one to another is in violation of scripture. The Lord would rather see this person out of the church, than one who has 'slipped'. The only treasure you can give from your heart is love. That is the only thing God will honor; things done and words spoken in love. Love is the only thing that truly changes a person. When you love a person, you make them feel like they are appreciated. You help them establish a good outlook toward themselves. You give them inner strength. You make them feel they are worth something to you, to God, to the world. You create change in that person by love, just like Jesus created change in you by His love. Paul also said, "We give no offense in anything that our ministry may not be blamed." (2 Cor.6:3)

How many times have we all committed sins which we have repented of and made our lives right with God? Those issues are then settled between you and God. In those cases how would you like someone to start speaking evil of you regarding sins which have been forgiven and forgotten by God and you? That person is committing the greater sin and standing in judgment before God. Jesus is the one who will judge the world in righteousness. (Acts 17:31) Don't forget that; and don't forget that when someone repents not only are they forgiven but they are cleansed from all unrighteousness. (1 Jn.1:9) Why are you trying to judge them when Jesus doesn't?

God's love is beyond reason. He ever hungers and yearns for the return of someone who sins. The righteous are already His. They have the Father's love. (i.e. the other son in the parable) Yet, sometimes the righteous become self-righteous and judgmental. This is detestable in God's eyes because they refuse to love with God's own love and rejoice over the return of someone who has sinned. The command by Jesus to love one another without respect of persons is a good and enjoyable command. It brings freedom not bondage to the human conscience. Are we serving one another with our attitudes and our words? Are we walking in the fruit of the Spirit? Are we showing the world there is something different in the way we treat each other in love? Love covers a multitude of sins. Don't just know it; practice it. If you don't, you are still walking in pure carnality and living out of your old sinful self.

AS IT IS IN HEAVEN

Meditate on the part of, 'The Lord's Prayer' that Jesus taught, "Your will be done on earth as it is in heaven." (Mt.6:10) Ask yourself if what you say, do, and feel about people now would be acceptable in heaven. It may shock you into some major attitude adjustments. Jesus repeated the same instruction in (Jn.17:21), "That they all may be one, as You Father, are in me, and I in You, that they also may be one in Us, that the world may believe that You sent Me." There is perfect unity between the Father and the Son. There is perfect unity in heaven. Therefore anything on earth which doesn't contribute to unity, especially in the church, is totally against God's word and will! In heaven we will be each other's servant for eternity, so are we considering the importance of how special your brothers and sisters in Christ are to you now? Doesn't the Bible say to consider each other better than yourself? "Let nothing be done through selfish ambition or conceit, but in lowliness of mind let each esteem others better than himself." (Phil.2:3) That is the heart of a servant, and one who will be considered by God to be the greatest in His kingdom. (Mt.23:11) All strife between people can be traced back to the most wickedness of sins, human pride. All problems between people are caused by what 'self' wants. But isn't that rotten, old bull-headed self supposed to be crucified with Christ, so the heart of a servant can be continually developed in the believer?

God hates violence and wickedness. He destroyed the world with water, save Noah and his family, because of the violence and wickedness in it. (Gen.6:5) Violence and wickedness which God hated was not limited to an act, but included thoughts of it. So, if you are thinking one single unforgiving or bad thought against someone you are committing wickedness. Why do you think scripture says our minds must be renewed? (Rom.12:2) I think God is more concerned about your mind than He is your actions, because actions are initiated by thoughts. That's why the apostle Paul wrote, "Let this mind be in you which was also in Christ Jesus." (Phil.2:5) He also wrote to the Corinthian church, "be of one mind, live in peace; and the God of love and peace will be with you." (2 Cor.13:11) So, when our thoughts are right, our words and actions will be right. He ended this second letter by saying, "The grace of the Lord Jesus Christ and the love of God and the communion of the Holy Spirit be with you all. Amen." (:14) This is God's will for all His believers. As we just obey the greatest two commandments, which include loving God with all your mind (Lk.10:27) this happens. Great revivals which produce great harvests come from great revivals of love!

BOUND IN SPIRIT

Just before the apostle, Paul, left Ephesus for Jerusalem toward the end of his last missionary journey he addressed the elders of that city saying, "And see now I go bound in the spirit to Jerusalem; not knowing the things that will happen to me there, except that the Holy Spirit testifies in every city saying that chains and tribulations await me. But none of these things move me; nor do I count my life dear to myself so that I may finish my race with joy, and the ministry which I received from the Lord Jesus to testify to the gospel of the grace of God." (Acts 20:22-24) Jesus told Paul the things he must suffer for the name of Jesus right from the beginning. (Acts 9:15,16) He knew trouble awaited him in Jerusalem. However, Paul did not deter from his call regardless of the things he suffered. He knew what his purpose was and remained determined to fulfill and complete it. God also told Joseph what the end result of his mission in life was. Joseph also endured much hardship, but saw the vision he had in his younger years fulfilled.

Being bound in the Spirit means you remain so tight with God, that you have His mind in all things. Then, like Paul, you refuse to be affected by the things in your life and ministry which would try to deter you. Paul did not count his own life important and dwell on the persecutions and abuse he suffered, so he could maintain his happiness with Jesus. Afflictions come in different forms, but are meaningless in comparison to the fruit produced as one stays bound in Spirit. Are we committed to self or to Jesus? If we are constantly mourning about how poor old self is hurt in one way or another we are not bound in Spirit, but still bound to self. Scripture records both Paul and Joseph felt they had no one to support them at times, but neither did this deter them. As the body of Christ individually and collectively stays determined to be bound in the Spirit, they remain bound in the love of God. The fourth man will be with them in every situation. As Jesus went around doing good, so shall His body move into every public arena and show forth the grace and power only Jesus can give. Salvations and miracles will be happening everywhere in everyday activities and associations. It is as good and as necessary to maintain the right attitude in fulfilling purpose as it is to fulfill purpose itself. Paul said even if he had faith to move mountains and had not love he was nothing. (1 Cor.13:2) God looks on the heart. When He sees everyone's faith working by love, God binds His Holy Spirit so tightly to ours, His anointing will be on us to break every yoke in private or in public. This is a witness to His love for all mankind. Amen.

GREATER THINGS

The human mind is a funny thing. When something is too good to be true, or too big to be considered, or too powerful to be understood the human mind often rejects it. Why? The human mind can't handle it. It never will because God's ways are not man's ways. In order to understand God's ways and what He says about His promises and facts in the Bible it must be taken by faith alone and acted on by faith alone.

There is one thing Jesus said when taken by faith alone will change your whole Christian outlook. The victory you have and the victory you can minister to others is based on this: "Most assuredly I say to you, He who believes in Me; the works that I do he will do also and greater works than these he will do because I go to My Father. And whatsoever you ask in My name that I will do that the Father may be glorified in the Son. If you ask anything in my name I will do it." (Jn.14:12-14) Of course you have asked yourself many times how could this be; that I could work greater works than Jesus? Maybe there is one thing you never considered. When Jesus said this it was before His crucifixion and before He went to hell and took the keys of death and hell back from the devil and gave them to the church. Jesus had walked through the streets and towns doing supernatural works and miracles because the devils had to obey Him, being God in the flesh. However, the power the devil had over all the earth had not yet been broken. Then He broke the power of death and hell after He said this and gave this new authority to the church, so, they could do even greater works. Now, all the devil's power has been rendered useless against the name of Jesus! He said this before the disciples were filled with the Holy Spirit to use this authority. After these two events the church was left to do the greater works evidenced by their works in the book of Acts.

Taking this to heart should give every believer the Holy Spirit mind-set to walk and live as much as possible in supernatural power over everything sinful, unhealthy and negative. The perspective you have on everything should be one of total positive overcoming power in Jesus name, for He is the one who is still accomplishing it all through us as we use the authority, HIS VERY OWN AUTHORITY, in His name. So, when you wake up in the morning it is right to say to yourself I may be doing some things greater than the works of Jesus, because He broke all the power of the devil after He said that, so I can live in total victory and minister the same to others. Just think of the privilege we have to continue the ministry of Jesus, but in even bigger and better ways. Think it, talk it, act it! You will see it!

HARVEST TIME

The apostle, Paul, said in (2 Cor.6:2), "Behold now is the accepted time, behold now is the day of salvation." Much of the church world is still waiting for God to do something He has commissioned the church to do. When Jesus spoke of harvest time in (Jn.4:35) He was very urgent in what He said, "Do you not say, There are still four months and then comes the harvest? Behold I say to you, Lift up your eyes, and look on the fields: for they are already white for harvest." When wheat is at the point of harvest it is a golden color. When it becomes white, it is not because it is ready to harvest, but it is ready to rot in the field. Jesus was actually telling His disciples they better harvest the crop immediately because it was at the point of rotting. The crop was beyond ripe! Time is short before His return. The word of God has become white in the hearts of many because there have been no harvesters. If the farmer is the one who plants the seed he is also the one who harvests it. You can't have one without the other or the whole crop is lost. The Old Testament prophet, Joel, in (1:17) said, "The seed is rotten under the clods, the garners are laid desolate, the barns are broken down, for the corn is withered." The word, 'withered', in the Hebrew means to be ashamed, confused, or disappointed. So, the word is rotten in many hearts, the depositories are devastated, the barns (churches) are broken down, all because the harvest is withered. We must change this by becoming harvesters while the crop is still golden.

In this day and age the Ten Commandments are not revered by the government or general public. In Joel's time the same was true. This brought the nation of Israel into destruction and exile. So, it has been with every empire since then which decayed internally. The word of God has never changed. Those who hold it close to their hearts and live it will be protected and held blameless before God. The whole church world is to blame for the harvest becoming white. The harvest of souls is beyond ripe in this world. Yet, how many churches are earnestly trying to evangelize their community instead of just setting up programs which may please themselves and those within their church? The harvest was beyond ripe in Jesus' time and it is beyond ripe now. Jesus said in the end time the love of many would wax cold. When Jesus saw how needy the people were to be saved, healed and fed, He was moved with compassion and acted in love. First He preached the kingdom of God, then He met needs. Where has the compassion gone for those who are hurting in or out of the church? It is time the church set an example as never before for the love of God to be made known. The kingdom of God must be preached and taught to everyone. When that happens, the work of the Holy Spirit will accomplish the expansion of it in many hearts, minds, and souls. The churches will become true harvesters and get the harvest before it turns white.

PRESENTING THE GOSPEL

The Bible says to know how to talk to all people. (Col.4:6) The way you present the gospel to one person may not be exactly the same way you present it to the next person. However, the bottom line is always the same; their need to accept Jesus. You do not have to say the exact same words in the sinner's prayer for every person. The way you present the gospel usually determines whether or not the person receives Jesus. What people want and need to know is how much they are loved by God through Jesus. If the gospel is presented in this light people are more apt to listen and receive. Just your general love for people is often enough to draw them to you and subsequently to Jesus. Living the love of Jesus brings God's wisdom to you in ministering. Jesus used words of knowledge to get the woman at the well saved. He used healing to get other people saved. Most important was the love He showed people in what He did.

Paul records in (2 Timothy 4:16-18), "At my first defense no one stood with me, but all forsook me: May it not be charged against them. But the Lord stood with me and strengthened me so that the message might be preached fully through me and that all the Gentiles might hear. Also I was delivered out of the mouth of the lion. And the Lord will deliver me from every evil work and preserve me for His heavenly kingdom. To Him be glory for ever and ever. Amen!" Paul had many opportunities to give up in his evangelistic efforts, but was determined his preaching was going to reach all the Gentiles. What motivated him? It had to be the love of God. He didn't want those who forsook him to be blamed as he reached out to a whole race of people who needed salvation. He showed love before and behind him. Sometimes God will require that of us; not only going forward in love, but going back in love which is sometimes the hardest. You will find out people will then not only be getting saved in front of you but also behind you. On the cross Jesus said, "Father, forgive them, for they do not know what they do."(Luke 23:34) When Stephen was stoned to death he prayed, "Lord, do not charge them with this sin." (Acts 7:60) The last thing Jesus and Stephen practiced just before they died was forgiveness.

God is love. (1 John 4:8) The spirit which made our spirit new is the spirit of love. Let us live the love of Jesus which is already inside us and that spirit will make our evangelism easy and fun.

RESURRECTION

If Jesus had not risen from the dead our faith would be futile. (1 Cor.15:17) But because He did, we also shall rise. Our faith should not only stand in our eternity, but in living the resurrected life here on earth. Jesus came to give us life and to give it in abundance. (Jn.10:10) Jesus destroyed death itself (2 Tim.1:10) and everything that leads to death. That's why in Him we can destroy everything in our life which would try to kill, steal or destroy any part of it. This is living the resurrected life now. That's how God wants us to live! He has given us everything we need to live it in Jesus.

You are a new person in Jesus. (2 Cor.5:17) Your own personal growth as a Christian depends on how much you want to develop that newness into something very beautiful for yourself and others. Stop spending time trying to improve your old person. You can't improve a dead person. Spend your time developing your new resurrected self which is now been made alive over your old self. Don't dwell on any past weaknesses or failures. Those items are dead, buried and forgotten with your old self. Identify with the new person God has made you through Jesus. This person is completely forgiven, healed, delivered, set free, loving, forgiving, and very powerful and anointed walking in the new life with Jesus. Learn to receive all these things in your character and life. They have been given. (Rom.8:32) A change of identity is required in order to realize and receive all the blessings which have been provided in Jesus. If you still have the same problems you haven't changed your identity in that situation and applied the Word needed to destroy that problem. The Bible says you can do all things through Christ who strengthens you. (Phil.4:13) If you still want to walk and try to achieve things in your own power God will allow that until you realize you can't. Then you will come to realize total surrender to the Lord does not make you weak, but makes you strong. You will understand being humble before God is a very powerful place to live. You will move into a place where His presence, His anointing is constantly active in your life no matter where you go or what you do. This is living the resurrected life. This is what makes you think, talk, respond, and live different. Everything in heaven in the final resurrection will have this difference. What did Jesus say in the Lord's prayer? "Be it on earth as it is in heaven." (Mt.6:10 kjv) Jesus was the Word and became flesh. (Jn.1:1,14) We are flesh and should become the Word. As it says in (1 Peter 4:11), "If anyone speaks, let him speak as the oracles of God......." This means applying the Word and truth of God to every situation and every circumstance in your life. You won't be disappointed. God watches over His word to perform it. The resurrected life is always in you in your spirit. This is the light which drives out darkness by your words and sometimes just by your presence. When you live the resurrected life, you can give the same resurrected life to others. Others see it and want it.

BEING SPIRITUALLY MINDED

In this hour the Lord is stressing the importance of staying filled with the Holy Spirit. Besides seeing the greatest manifestations of God's glory, staying filled prevents you from being deceived. It's a fight, "against principalities, against powers, against the rulers of the darkness of this age, against spiritual hosts of wickedness in the heavenly places." (Eph. 6:12) The devil is the deceiver. (Rev.20:8) When you get saved you are forgiven from all sin in your life, but not necessarily totally delivered from the power behind the sin. Demons will still try to oppress your mind and body. If you say there in no temptation in your life to make you think and act sinfully, demons have a right to remain and will. The apostle, John, was writing to Christians when he said, "If we say that we have no sin we deceive ourselves and the truth is not in us." (1 John 1:8) You must want to overcome and get rid of all demon spirits and their thoughts no matter how long you have identified with them as being part of you and your thoughts. They are not! This is probably one of the most important times in your Christian walk to be humble before God and repent. The devil has tricked you into believing his thoughts are your thoughts. When you continue to discern what is really going on, then get delivered, you will find out who the real 'you' is in Jesus. You will continue to like yourself more, for you will see yourself being more transformed into the image of His Son, changing from glory to glory, with more of the active presence of God in your life. People will take notice. The best person to deliver you is yourself. You know yourself better than anyone else does except God. The best way to discern whether or not you are being oppressed is to ask yourself, "Would Jesus be thinking, acting, or talking like this?" If you stay filled with the Holy Spirit, it's very easy to fight this battle and be a winner because you are keeping the greater power in you constantly active.

If you hear negative comments like, "That's just the way I am.", or, "I've always been like that." the person has been deceived. The flesh always has and always will hate the Holy Spirit. However, when we make a conscious decision we are going to do everything God's way we find out how rich life can really be.

The Bible says:

(Romans 12:1,2) "I beseech you therefore, brethren, by the mercies of God that you present your bodies a living sacrifice, holy, acceptable to God which is your reasonable service. And do not be conformed to this world but be transformed by the renewing of your mind; that you may prove what is that good and acceptable and perfect will of God."

(Phil.2:5) "Let this mind be in you which was also in Christ Jesus." How much of the mind of Christ you want is up to you.

(1 Cor. 2:10-16) Rd. There is no other foundation of truth except that which is laid by the Spirit, and no other basis of instruction except that which is taught by the Spirit with the mind of Christ according to the word of God.

(Romans 8:4-8) Rd. The more filled with the Spirit you are, the more pleasing you are to God. Carnal mindedness is separation from God.

(Romans 6 Rd. all especially 10,11,12) "For the death that he died, He died to sin once for all; but the life that he lives, he lives to God. Likewise you also reckon yourselves to be dead indeed to sin, but alive to God in Christ Jesus our Lord."

FAITH AND TRUST

(Psalm 37:5) "Commit your way to the Lord, Trust also in Him and He shall bring it to pass." Faith is believing. You believe God because you trust Him and his word. Faith is built on trust. Buts, ifs, maybes, outside God's word are not in God's vocabulary and shouldn't be in ours. God's word is true. (Jn.8:31,32), (Psalm 119:160) It never changes. (Isaiah 40:8) God stands true to His word to perform it. (Rom.4:21) If you don't have complete trust in God, don't expect to receive anything from Him. (James 1:6,7) Trust in God means letting the word of God become more real to you than the circumstances over which it relates to (sickness, sin, temptations, oppressions, poverty, etc.) Living with and walking out the word in your life gives you the revelation that the natural circumstances and conditions have absolutely no bearing on God's ability which is so much greater. Trust in God sees your work for Him through to completion on every level. Trust in God sees the answers to prayer manifested. As your trust in God increases, you are depending more on Him, His words, and His abilities; not on yourself, your words and abilities. Receiving what the Bible says about simply trusting God will increase your faith. You see, it is faith in God that works, not faith in yourself.

(Rom. 4:17-21) and (Psalm 37:5) line up. Abraham's faith based on complete trust in what God had spoken made Abraham fully persuaded that what God had promised he was able to perform. (:21) The very same principle based on complete trust in God is for us too. (:22-24) Who says we can't have the same kind of faith as Abraham? Trust God and you will through Jesus.

Products of trust:

(2 Sam.22:31) "...He is a shield to all who trust in Him."

(1 Chron. 5:20) "…for they cried out to God in the battle. He heeded their prayer because they put their trust in Him."

(Psalm 2:12) "Blessed are all those who put their trust in Him."

(Psalm 5:11) "But let all those rejoice who put their trust in You, Let them ever shout for joy because You defend them."

(Psalm 9:10) "And those who know Your name will put their trust in You, for You, Lord, have not forsaken those who seek You."

(Psalm 16:1) "Preserve me O God, for in You I put my trust."

(Psalm 17:7) "...O You who save those who put their trust in You."

(Psalm 18:30) "...He is a shield to all who trust in Him."

(Psalm 25:20) "Keep my soul and deliver me; Let me not be ashamed, for I put my trust in You."

(Psalm 31:19) "Oh, how great is Your goodness…, Which you have prepared for those that trust in You."

(Psalm 34:22) "...none of those who trust in Him shall be condemned."

(Psalm 37:3 kjv) "Trust in the Lord, and do good so shall you dwell in the land and verily be fed."

(Psalm 37:40) "And the Lord shall help them and deliver them; He shall deliver them from the wicked And save them Because they trust in him."

(Psalm 40:4) "Blessed is that man who makes the Lord his trust..."

(Psalm 62:8) "Trust in Him at all times; you people, pour out your heart before Him; God is a refuge for us."

(Psalm 71:1) "In You, O Lord, I put my trust; Let me never be put to shame."

(Psalm 73:28) "...I have put my trust in the Lord God, That I may declare all Your works."

These are but a few of the benefits in trusting God. Faith believes, speaks, acts and receives. This is done in trust. That's why there is no room for fear or confusion, no matter how long it takes to get your answer. Faith and trust always bring victory!

CONSCIENCE

Your conscience is inborn. It is the standard within by which you determine right and wrong on every issue toward self and God. When your conscience is kept free and true before God it is very easy to work with, respond to, and enjoy the Holy Spirit's presence. Likewise, it is very easy to work with and minister to people with God's help. Nothing is blocking you from receiving from God, giving out the things of God, and communing with the Lord.

Every since the fall of Adam and Eve, the human conscience has been perverted. "...the time is coming that whosoever kills you will think that he offers God service. And these things they will do to you because they have not known the Father nor me." (Jn.16:2,3) Without being born again, the human conscience is still perverted. Wrong will seem right, sinful pleasure will seem good, and true righteousness in Jesus will be scoffed at. However, when one truly gets saved, the human conscience bears witness to the Holy Spirit's leading in all things and one's conscience can be kept clear from the clutter which has prevented you from really living free in Jesus. Paul said, "...I myself always strive to have a conscience without offense toward God and men." (Acts 24:16) He also wrote to Timothy, "Now the purpose of the commandment is love from a pure heart, from a good conscience, and from sincere faith." (1 Tim.1:5) Paul knew the importance of having his mind clear so, the anointing on his life could be effective. That is why it is so important to live with all sin confessed and repented of under the blood of Jesus; and with the mind-set of forgiveness and being forgiven toward yourself and others. For it is there your mind is not troubled. It is there you can be so free with people, not having offenses or mistakes in your mind drawing on the flow of God's love and Holy Spirit in you.

If you spend time trying always to improve yourself, you won't. You or the devil will always show you one more thing about self which isn't right. However, when you spend time devoted to and engaged in the things of God your mind and conscience is on Jesus. You don't have the time thinking much about self. The best way to keep a clean conscience is just serving God. The process of keeping a clean heart happens by itself because your heart is with God, not yourself. The process of being conformed to the image of Jesus also happens by itself by serving Him. The change doesn't happen all at once. It's from glory to glory. But it is accelerated by having a strong attraction to the righteousness of God which is in Christ Jesus. We all have to live with ourselves. The best way to stay happy and strong is simply by loving God and people. Our conscience remains free and clear; our spirit in touch with Jesus!

OUTLOOK

How is your outlook on life? Is your glass half-empty or is it half-full? If it is half-empty soon you will be very thirsty and dry. If it's half-full, soon you will be well-watered and overflowing. The choice is yours not God's. He wants us to live with an expectation for the very best in life. "I have come that they may have life and that they may have it more abundantly." (Jn.10:10) Much of that 'may' and 'more' involves our outlook. Joshua and Caleb knew they could take the Promised Land with God's help. Forty-five years later Caleb's outlook never changed. Hebron was conquered and inherited by Caleb. He said, "Now, therefore give me this mountain.....It may be that the Lord will be with me and I shall be able to drive them out as the Lord said." (Josh.14:12) There was no fear, only confidence in Caleb's outlook. He got what he wanted because the Lord was with him. "If God is for us who could be against us?" (Rom. 8:31)

When you allow God to direct and orchestrate your life you will get the same results as Caleb. But that requires you walk according to the Word and Spirit. I think too many people try to claim God's promises and provisions without doing that, then end up blaming God when things don't turn out right. Those people must ask themselves how much of their flesh and own human will was involved in it from the beginning. If they are then honest with themselves they will realize it was their own fault, not God's. Then, if they choose to do it God's way according to His Word and Spirit things will change for the better, but not until. Even though there is so much liberalism in today's mind-set, God's principles and absolutes in His Word never change and must be followed if the blessing is to be expected. Even though the world is so full of excuses, blame-fixing, denial, and lack of absolute thinking, that will never change the requirements God expects to be met in order for the fullness of His blessings to be realized. But, it is surely worth the time, effort, and patience it takes to be obedient because when God sees a heart like that He often will bless far beyond our own expectations. How many times does it have to be said about the heart being in the right condition before God? It is well worth any sacrifice made because it is a sacrifice for something better. You lose nothing except your pride and you gain everything with humbleness before God. The worldly rational mind will resist that type of outlook; but neither does it understand living by faith. It is by faith a Christian chooses to be obedient, and put away childish things. Then their life is lived with full-blown confidence God and all of heaven are backing them up in everything they do. Confidence and boldness become a constant in their life. Fear and doubt are complete strangers and afraid to come around. Real love from God is felt everyday because He gets pleasure from obedient people and rewards them.

LOGIC

Yes, the just shall live by faith. (Gal.3:11) There is a whole lot of logical reasoning and conclusions about why one should live by faith. When one takes God's word as fact about how well the Bible works; about how good God is; about what the end result of faith in Jesus as Lord and Savior will be in this life and the next, <u>it is just plain logical</u> to live by faith. It is not a questionable activity. It is simply how to live the best life you can have with God's abilities going so far beyond your own. Without living by faith you limit yourself. You will only go as far as human abilities allow. That's not much. When you allow God to be seriously active in your life there is no limit to what can be accomplished for God and yourself. <u>That's logical</u>. Faith is not a wild, hair-brained, fanatical, emotional response. Living by faith and <u>USING GOD'S WORD TO BE ACTIVE IN YOUR LIVE</u> is the most logical thing a person could do once they know Jesus and claim to be a Christian.

Everything in the end will be in God. (1 Cor.15:28) After all the shaking stops and evil is no more, God's people will enjoy the benefits of a faith life they now live. If the Bible says you are going to be joint-heirs with Jesus isn't it logical to be thankful and worshipful to God now? Isn't it logical to let the supernatural life come into your natural life now? Every time one lets the flesh rule it is illogical. That is not who you are, nor is it even using common sense. Believing God for the impossible is common sense for the Christian. Being joyful and happy amidst trying circumstances is a natural response to the things which would try to drag you from your relationship with Jesus. <u>It's just logical</u> to shout praises to our Lord as Paul and Silas did in prison. It's just logical to call those things which be not as though they were. You are operating on truth which will always be truth. Your foundation in life is different from the world's foundation. You act, think, and live differently because <u>it's the logical thing to do</u>. Do you want God to recognize you as His own in this world? The different life style will become normal and as you mature in Jesus it will seem illogical to live any other way. What is common sense and logical with God is something the world regards as foreign and fanatical. So what? It's great to live the difference. As Christians we are different because of an active God in us which we are supposed to let control our mind and body. When we live our life like that it is logical to expect miracle power and supernatural things happening all around us on a daily basis. It is logical to live with a 24/7 activated God in our life. It's logical to expect to be so much different because of the love and power of God in us, so the world can see the difference and want what we have, JESUS! JESUS! JESUS! JESUS! JESUS! JESUS! JESUS! JESUS! JESUS!

IMAGE AND LIKENESS

(Gen.1:26) Then God said, "Let us make man in Our image, according to our likeness; let them have dominion..." There's a very strong point to be made here. All people, saved and unsaved are created in God's image, spiritual people whether or not they want to admit it. Adam and Eve were originally created in His image and likeness. They were spiritual beings and before the fall had the likeness of God. After they sinned and contaminated the human race with the sin nature, people were still created in His image, but not His likeness. The word likeness infers and implies the very manner or character of God, not just the form or image. So, what does all this mean?

It means a person's spirit has to be born-again in order to regain God's likeness. God is more concerned about forming a Godly character in His people than He is about leaving them in comfort without Godly character development. Why do you think we are tested? The fruit of the Spirit, love, joy, peace, long-suffering, gentleness, goodness, faith, meekness and temperance (Gal.5:22) does not come without the Spirit; and the Spirit does not come without being born-again. God is love. (1 Jn.4:8) As a Christian, everything one does is worthless unless it's done by love. This is where the likeness of God is developed. You are created in His image, but now you must be developed in His likeness. I think God wanted us to know from the first chapter of Genesis, He was not just an image, or a thing, or a religious article. He wanted us to know He is a loving, spiritual, emotional being with character and personality; someone who needs to be loved, praised, appreciated and worshiped for all He has done for us through love in Jesus. So, we, in turn, should form our character to His likeness in loving and giving. It is then we are supposed to have dominion according to this statement of creation. First comes the image, then likeness, then dominion. Just think if God told the human race to take dominion without His likeness being developed first? What a terrible representation of Him we would make. I think God will not let anyone operate under a large amount of His spiritual authority unless His love is developed in that person first. Before being an ambassador of power He calls us to be ambassadors of His love. Why are we commanded to walk in love without option? He wants His true likeness represented in this world. The world isn't impressed just because you tell them you are a Christian. They will want what you have when they see, feel, hear and experience God's unconditional love being extended to them. You are showing them your likeness to God. So, let us all work on that likeness. People are more attracted to love than anything else.

GOD'S GREATNESS

God created all things. I observed an insect hopping on the rail of my back porch the other day and thought about how that one insect related to birds and flowers and how God arranged that. Then I thought about the sun and how God put it at the perfect distance from the earth to help support life. Then I thought about how many trillions of light years the universe is, and how God measured it with the span of His hand, (i.e. thumb to little finger, Isaiah 40:12). After considering how big and intelligent God is, I straight out said to Him I can in no way even begin to comprehend how great you really are. I am absolutely nothing, nothing at all in myself before you. I considered the beautiful colors of the tropical fishes and how His divine intelligence makes everything in life work. After all this meditation I admitted to God and myself that even on the best of my best days how much I still fall short. It wasn't a matter of self-incrimination, guilt, or condemnation. Jesus paid the price for all of that and made me new in His eyes as He did you. But it was a matter of becoming humble before God out of reverence and asking Him to completely break me into little pieces if there was just one piece out of order. It felt great becoming totally vulnerable before God. He loves honesty. It reminded me of the scripture in (Psm.51:17), "The sacrifices of God are a broken spirit, a broken and contrite heart, These, O God, You will not despise." Also (1 Cor.10:12) "Therefore let him who thinks he stands, take heed lest he fall." So, I continued to talk to God. I told Him you know all the good and all the bad parts. I said I remain humble before you and helpless without your grace and mercy. I totally depend on you for everything and trust you for everything in my life. It feels like you cleanse yourself when you can become totally honest about yourself before God. Nothing is hidden with Him anyway. You know there are still some things about self which are not right. But when you become totally honest before God you will feel a release and put yourself in a position God can really use you. This is because as you continue to give yourself to God daily in all things, it will be Himself in operation when you minister. The judgment of our sins was upon Jesus. You have been made the righteousness of God in Him, but only in Him, not yourself. It is only in Him you remain righteous before God. That's why Paul said he had to die daily to self. Pride is the worst of sins because it is the one thing which will keep you from being humble, honest before God. It is necessary to experience the value in our heart of staying very vulnerably before God in everything. It is there we are cleansed, forgiven, have peace of mind and conscience, and are useable.

COMMUNICATION

Almost all personal problems between people are based on a lack of communication. Great personal relationships are based on excellent communication. The greater a relationship becomes due to spoken communication. It goes to a new level when spoken communication isn't always needed because the people know each other so well, they know without speaking. Unity and communication with the Holy Spirit works like this. God set up the same order for us. First, He has spoken and communicated to us by His Word, the Bible. We read and study His Word and communicate His Word back to Him in prayer, praise and fellowship. His Words are Spirit and life. (Jn.6:63) The longer we spend hearing and communicating with Him by His Word, the sooner we can expect that connection in the Holy Spirit where we can see and know unspoken things. The apostle, Paul, prayed that God would give us, "the spirit of wisdom and revelation in the knowledge of Him, the eyes of your understanding being enlightened that you may know..." (Eph.1:17,18) God is Spirit and they that worship Him must worship Him in Spirit and in truth. First God wants us to live according to His Word as a guideline. Then His direction to us is by the Holy Spirit. Communication between the Son and the Father is spiritual. Communication between the Holy Spirit and Jesus is spiritual. Communication between the Holy Spirit and us is spiritual. Let's get all human reasoning out of the formula between us, God, and each other. The Holy Spirit is called the spirit of truth, (Jn.14:17, 16:13) because He receives from Jesus who is also the truth. (Jn.14:6)

We have no options to live contrary to the Word which is truth. The devil is always a deceiver and will try to make you live a lie. Any lie you live breaks communication between you and the one who saved you. Jesus said anyone who loves Him and keeps His words, both Jesus and the Father will live with him. (Jn.14:23) Also, they that are led by the Spirit, they are the sons of God. (Rom.8:14) Walk in the light with the Word and Spirit.

LIVING IN CHANGE

"The joy of the Lord is your strength." (Neh.8:10) "But he who is of a merry heart has a continual feast." (Prov.15:15) God doesn't just want us to get saved. He wants us to live in the experience of salvation everyday of our life. It's the feeling you get as if you never broke the first great kiss you ever had. That's how God wants us to live with and in Him.

You know there is a big change in you once you are born-again. That wasn't just an experience. A permanent change happened when you let Jesus into your spirit. God wants you to live in the experience of that change every day of your life. He wants you to enjoy the experience of His love, forgiveness and mercy on a daily basis. The early church, "...continued steadfastly in the apostles' doctrine and fellowship in the breaking of bread and in prayers." (Acts 2:42), "And they continued daily with one accord in the temple and breaking bread from house to house they ate their food with gladness and simplicity of heart." (:46) It says the gladness resided in their heart daily. They didn't just experience Jesus. They experienced a daily gladness because they chose to live in the way Jesus changed them. They knew they were loved by God in a way which was beyond words. That love produced change. Then they lived in that change. Love will always produce change.

The same is true for us. We must choose to live in that change. That means a whole lot of new things. You now see yourself as a person who is valuable and loved by Jesus. He was willing to die for you so you can respond to life in a whole lot of different ways. Your identity is now different from anything in the world. You no longer have to identify yourself as the person you once were. That change in you is so permanently good you no longer are that person. Your whole mental outlook will change from weakness, insecurity and mistrust to strength, security and power because God Himself now lives in you. You are defined by what you commit yourself to, so, you, as a Christian, choose to live in the big change which has made you a new person. You have a new life. The blessings of God will be constant. How much your life is changed depends on how much you want to live in that change. That part is up to us.

"Therefore your gates shall be open continually; they shall not be shut day or night..." (Isaiah 60:11) We will be living in the permanent environment of God's permanent love for us with permanent access to His greatness and strength for all of eternity. All of that is already in us in Jesus. As we commit ourselves to the change which is already in us all of the wrong attitudes and actions will seem foreign. We act, live and think different because we are different. Jesus made us different. We no longer belong to ourselves. We are God's property created to be like Him. Let us live in that process of change.

HIM ONLY SHALL YOU SERVE

First the devil tried to tempt Jesus to submit to what was appealing to the flesh when he said, "If You are the Son of God command this stone to become bread." (Lk.4:3) Obviously Jesus was hungry after fasting forty days. When that didn't work he tried to tempt Jesus with what was appealing to the intellect or 'soul realm' when he offered Jesus the 'kingdoms of the world', (:5). This part of a person is what the devil is really after because it's based on self and controls the flesh part of the person. You see, Satan is based totally on himself and wants to make people like that. He tried his best to make pride well up in Jesus by tempting Him to cast himself down from the pinnacle of the temple. (:9) He tried to make Jesus think He could do anything He wanted to just because He was the Son of God. That didn't work either. Jesus stayed totally out of the realm of 'self' in everything He did right up to the cross. When His intellect or 'soul realm' was tested He said, "Get behind me, Satan, for it is written, <u>You shall worship the Lord your God, and him only you shall serve</u>." (:8) How many times do we as Christians still say and do things which are pleasing to our intellect instead of giving that part of ourselves to God? I believe that sin is even worse than committing a sin of the flesh, for the former is based totally on self which is totally against God; the later is based on pleasing the carnal nature we are born with. Don't be confused. Both are wrong; but remember what happened to the man who wanted to build bigger barns so everyone would know how great he was. That night he died. (Lk.12:16-21) It says <u>he was first talking to his own soul</u>, then getting ready to please his flesh with all his goods. (:19) I often wonder how long it's going to take for Christians to realize that submission brings reward far beyond that which any human hand could supply. It says, "let us not grow weary while doing good, for in due season we shall reap <u>if we do not lose heart</u>." (Gal.6:9) Too many people either stop serving the Lord like they know they should, or decrease in the intensity they had when they got started and still expect all these great rewards. It doesn't work like that. Jesus said, "If anyone does not abide in Me, he is cast out as a branch and is withered..." (Jn.15:6) Maybe you are comfortable with all Biblical head knowledge and comfortable associations, but are doing nothing to win souls or fulfill your calling. You can still be serving self in that 'comfortable' place. We are living in a time God wants His people to rise up and go forth like a mighty army every day of their lives. His divine nature will become so strong on the inside of you nothing will stop the Word from producing fruit. You will shine in the presence of darkness and you will walk as the 'children of light', (Eph.5:8) and bring as many people as possible to Jesus before His return.

FLESH AND SPIRIT

One of the greatest mistakes we make as Christians is trying to fight the spiritual battle with the flesh. Oftentimes we don't even know that's what we are doing. The best way to add strength to an unresolved problem, attitude or temptation is to concentrate on it and try to figure out ways to fix it yourself. Your human will may give you temporary relief, but unless you let the Holy Spirit strengthen you in that area the problem will remain unresolved. Why does the Bible say, "Therefore submit to God. Resist the devil and he will flee from you." (James 4:7) It's because God wants you to overcome a lesser spirit with a greater one. This is something you cannot do in your own strength. It takes much discipline to stay absorbed in God and the kingdom of God. The quality of your Christian life is determined by how well you do this. But this is something you must do unless you want the temptations and ways of the world to flood your life and hinder your walk with God. The best way to overcome is to immediately refocus your attention on the things of God and keep your attention there, not on the problem. The Bible even tells us what to think about and what to do. The apostle, Paul, in writing to the Philippians said, "Finally brethren, whatever things are true, whatever things are noble, whatever things are just, whatever things are pure, whatever things are lovely, whatever things are of good report, if there is any virtue, if there is anything praiseworthy, meditate on these things. The things which you have learned, and received, and heard, and saw in me, these do, and the peace of God will be with you." (Phil.4:8,9) This takes a continual attitude of worship in your heart at all times, so the enemy cannot gain any ground in your thought life. We know our greatest enemy is ourselves. That's why we must continue to submit ourselves to God, His Word, His spirit. God has ways of showing you His wonderful grace and favor. As we choose to live in the life of the Spirit, the fruit of the Spirit, the gifts of the Spirit in our spirit, the favor of God in our life will be known. We will be strengthened and loved by God and others as this choice is made on a daily basis. You will see God continually opening doors for you to serve Him, mostly by serving others.

As said before, love attracts. Love is of the Spirit, not the flesh. Faith works by love, so submission to God is submission to love. Love strengthens you and is returned to you as you use it. A beautiful mutual dependence is developed between you and God. While this is going on a continual restraining order is issued to the devil and all his host. Just win the battle over self and everything else falls in place.

PREPARATION

In the fast-paced world we live in often our actions are not preceded with enough preparation. So it is in the ministry at times. Basic confusion is the product of either misinformation or not enough of the right information. First, you have to know what is required to be an effective minister. Any born-again, spirit-filled Christian is a minister of God. You don't have to fill an office. We all can be spiritual giants if we are prepared.

First, the right attitude is required. You must be willing to operate in love. You must not carry unforgiveness, or a hard spirit. Your channels to God must remain open with all sin confessed and under the blood. Then you can be led by the Holy Spirit and be spontaneous with God in your daily walk. The early church had to stay filled with the Holy Spirit on a daily basis because they knew nothing happened without the work of the Holy Spirit. Your ministry must line up with the fact that you have been given the power over all power of the enemy and be confident in the fact nothing will harm you. (Lk.10:19) This will eliminate fear and give you confidence to persist regardless of any resistance. When Jesus taught His disciples how to pray He said, "Your kingdom come Your will be done on earth as it is in heaven." (Mt.6:10) This is directly related to the correct meaning of binding and loosing. Jesus taught, "…Whatever you bind on earth will be bound in heaven and whatever you loose on earth will be loosed in heaven." (Mt.18:18) The original Greek meaning of this is to declare illegal and unlawful on earth the things which have already been declared illegal and unlawful in heaven; and to declare legal and lawful on earth the things which have already been declared legal and lawful in heaven. The same principle is recorded in (Rom.4:17), "calls those things which do not exist as though they did." Therefore, this is not a practice of doing something to achieve something. It is an authoritative declaration of something which has already been done! It has already been accomplished in heaven. Therefore, our thoughts and words should not contain even one syllable of negativity especially in ministry because that has already been forbidden in heaven and will block the manifestation of the blessing on earth. The keys of the kingdom are based on a totally positive outlook. Otherwise your thoughts and words can declare the bad things legal in your life. They have already been declared illegal and disallowed. God really wants us to live and to give out the abundant life He has given us. This is done totally by faith alone in believing what He has promised He is able to perform. (Rom.4:21)

HOPE SHONE

(1 Pet. 3:15), "But sanctify the Lord God in your hearts and always be ready to give a defense to everyone who asks you a reason for *the hope that is in you,* with meekness and fear." The hope in us, the eternal God of glory, Jesus, must be revealed to the public. This scripture states the new life you have in Jesus should be so obvious people will be asking you about it and you should be ready to evangelism them all the time wherever you go! Otherwise you are no different than the unbeliever.

The book of Acts is totally evangelistic and is a model for the present day church. On the day of Pentecost three thousand souls got saved. (Acts 2:41) Then souls were added to the church daily. (:47) The joy of fellowship, worship, praise and prayer was absolutely not an end in itself. It was carried into the streets for people to get saved. Persecution led to more boldness. More boldness in public, not within the four walls of a church, led to great power and great grace with God. It won't come any other way. They received it when they were giving witness of the resurrection of the Lord. (4:33) All that dwelt at Lydda and Sharon who saw Aeneas healed turned to the Lord. (9:35) When Peter raised Tabitha from the dead many throughout Joppa believed. (9:42) If you received a healing from Jesus tell people about it. Many Jews and religious converts followed Paul and the word was published throughout the whole region. (13:43,49) At Iconium, a great multitude of the Jews and the Greeks believed. (14:1) On Paul's second missionary journey, the churches were strengthened in the faith and increased in number daily. (16:5)

The primary purpose of the church is to evangelize! It's to grow outward not inward with a self-centered mindset. How some church movements have changed the perspective on things. Some born-again people come to church to get their 'spiritual fix' for the day or the week, enjoy the presence of God for a moment, then could care less whether or not their neighbor is going to hell. Forms of worship, praise and prayer become the object of worship and devotion in order to get a 'feel good' feeling for the day or the week with absolutely no thought for the lost. The activities and programs which are not evangelistic should not outweigh the ones which are. I believe God commands a correction in Christian thinking and activity. The great commission of winning every soul you can to Jesus is our greatest commission. All other activity should contribute toward this end in one way or another. Stay filled so you can show the glory of the Lord which is in you to the world. It's very easy to see each other's light, but the world needs it more. We are the only true light they see.

JUST OR UNJUST

Sometimes scriptures relate facts, sometimes principles. When a scripture relates a principle it can be applied as truth to many different activities. It can stand as God's absolute truth in every one of them. "He who is faithful in what is least is faithful also in much; and he who is unjust in what is least is unjust also in much." (Lk..16:10) If you obey God in your own Christian life, it will grow in stature, wisdom, and power. God will not give you any large responsibilities until you have proven to be faithful in what you know is right. (James 4:17) "Therefore, to him who knows to do good and does not do it, to him it is sin." (2 Peter 3:17) "You, therefore; beloved, since you know this beforehand, beware lest you also fall from your own steadfastness being led away with the error of the wicked." Serving God means putting Him, His word, His principles first in every situation. Your decisions and actions should follow. Otherwise you are trying to serve people bringing unrighteous compromising into both your life and theirs. When you compromise with people in order not to offend them you are offending God. So, who would you rather offend, people or God? Scripture clearly states we are accountable for what we know and should adhere to it. A small amount of compromise will lead to more and destruction will follow. God will not violate His absolutes regardless of how much people think their way is right. It's not if it violates God's word in any way. There is a very steep price to pay if God has given you deep revelation and knowledge. You live with a hurt because you see so much compromise and deception. You live with the ideology of heaven in your spirit, but face the reality of error all around you. You see what God requires is so much different than man's opinion in and out of church. Your prayers and thoughts are internalized because nobody would understand you if you prayed out loud. You see people and things failing because even though they know the truth, they are not living it. Some false teachings and attitudes in the church have pulled God down, demanding Him to meet them at their own human comfort levels. They want to stay comfortable in their sins without feeling guilty about their errors. It doesn't work like that. As the blessings can grow in one's life, so can the curses depending on how close one adheres to God's absolutes. God always wants to bless, prosper, heal, provide and guide us. But He will not do it outside His own word and principles. When a person really wants to surrender it will cost them everything 'self' stands for. But, when you lose your life for Jesus' sake and the gospel's you will save it. (Mark 8:35)

HEAVEN

Jesus said, "...I go to prepare a place for you.... That where I am there you may be also." (Jn.14:2,3) As we are continually under construction, being built up into the likeness of Jesus on earth, so is heaven continually under construction at the hand of the master builder, Jesus. Mansions are not the only thing being built in heaven. If God wants to make room for another million angels and saints to dance on the sea of glass at the rapture of the church He will expand it. If He wants a million more instruments playing in heaven's band when the trumpet sounds He will make more instruments and train more players. Heaven is getting ready to throw the greatest party that ever was or will be. Tons of diamonds, emeralds and jewels, magnificent tapestries and decorations beyond the human imagination are daily being prepared for this great event in heaven. The bride of Christ, His church, will soon be caught up to be with the Lord at the great marriage supper of the Lamb. (Rev. 19:7)

Just before this happens God is going to push open the floodgates of heaven and cause the River of Life, His Spirit, His glory, to cover the earth. Then the earth is going to shake and crack to let the dead in Christ to come out of the grave and go up first. That very power, the resurrection power, is constantly on the increase in the world today. The presence of God, the anointing, is the resurrection power which will someday be turned on to such a degree it will draw God's people right up to heaven. Then shall we ever be with the Lord. God is spirit and everything in heaven is controlled by Him. When Jesus said to His disciples to pray for His will to be done on earth as it is in heaven do you realize how much He expects us to walk in the Spirit? He said they that are led by the Spirit are the sons of God. While on earth God wants us to carry the resurrection power with us wherever we go and just let Jesus be Himself in and through us in our words and deeds. The apostle, John, said in (Jn. 1:16), "And of His fullness we have all received and grace for grace." Paul wrote to the Colossians, "For in Him dwells all the fullness of the Godhead bodily. and, you are complete in Him...." (Col. 2:9,10) We will live in the resurrection power for all of eternity, but God wants us to live in it everyday of our lives. It exciting to be an active, not side-line Christian taking 'faith chances' wherever we go. Heaven will be our home, but we can pull down a little bit of heaven into our lives, and live in that place only you and God know about. So, let's live the resurrected life now. It will be ours for eternity!

LACKING NOTHING

Many things in the Old Testament are a type and shadow of things in the New Testament. When King David returned to Ziklag after winning the battle against the Amalekites who had originally plundered his camp he returned with everything which was stolen and more <u>lacking nothing.</u> (1 Sam. 30:19, 20) When Jesus gave us the resurrected life it was His very own resurrected life given us. Don't separate your thinking from that fact. When you consider the total victory He had accomplished over the devil and all his works and the same victory was given us in His resurrected life, you can rise up and recover everything which was robbed from you before salvation. You don't have to be anyone 'special' to receive everything which has been freely given us. Even the two hundred men who watched the goods when David went to battle got exactly equal shares of the spoil. (:21-25) From that day forward it was made a statute and an ordinance for that practice to continue. So it is from the day a person gets saved. What Jesus has done for us has never changed. It only gets better the more you realize it. God wants us to continue to grow in His grace. This is the age of His grace. When Peter wrote his second letter to the Corinthians in Asia Minor he said, "Grace and peace be multiplied to you in the knowledge of God and of Jesus, our Lord." (2 Pet.1:2) In the next verse he says, "…His divine power has given to us all things that pertain to life and godliness through the knowledge of Him who called us by glory and virtue." Then in the next verse he says we have been given, "exceeding great and precious promises that through these you may be partakers of the divine nature, having escaped the corruption that is in the world through lust." Then in verses (:5-7) he lists the virtues by which a person grows in grace, i.e. faith, virtue, knowledge, temperance, patience, godliness, brotherly kindness, and charity. He says if you are diligent about doing these things you shall never fail (:10) and that "an entrance shall be ministered to you abundantly into the everlasting kingdom of our Lord and Savior Jesus Christ." (:11)

In short what Peter is saying that to grow in grace you must grow in the knowledge of Jesus Christ. Then when you apply that knowledge God will perform what He has promised. God wants us to live life in abundance, not in lack. Knowledge alone won't bring you abundance. If you don't know how to apply the knowledge ask God to give you the wisdom how to. Then you will be like David who encouraged himself in the Lord, got the wisdom needed, went forth, won the battle, and returned <u>lacking nothing</u>. (1 Sam.30:6-8)

NEWNESS

What are people attracted too? Usually it's something new and exciting. Underneath many of the mental processes a demand for change is constantly at work. I believe that's a God-given phenomenon of the human mind. He made it like that to create an inner need for Himself in every person. Once the human spirit is born-again by the Holy Spirit that need is met. However, that specific need is still hungry for more and more of Him. Each level of faith has its' own satisfaction and its' own level of excitement for a while. Once a Christian learns to live on that level there is still a need for the next level and then the next or else their walk with the Lord can become boring.

So what is our responsibility as Christians? First it's to show the unsaved the newness in us. How can we expect the lost to want something they don't see in us? We are a new person in Jesus; new in love and new in supernatural power. We must show the world the same works that Jesus did. In (Matt. 16:18) Jesus said that by the prophetic, revelation anointing He would build His church and the gates of hell would not prevail against it. Gates don't attack. They don't even move. They are designed to keep something contained. What Jesus is really saying is the church will attack the gates, go in and release the captives, and the gates don't have a chance to stop us. We can and should unlock the gates with the keys of the kingdom given us. (Mt. 16:19) These are the same keys Jesus took from the devil. (Rev. 1:18) Once the church world realizes this and lives with the compassion of the Good Samaritan (Lk. Chap. 10) who is represented as Jesus, Himself, in this parable, churches will be filled to overflowing. The man who was beaten and robbed represents fallen mankind. When you reach new levels in faith and in Spirit you reach new levels of compassion. The deeper and higher you go with God the more the world will know the newness in you. As the angels circling the throne keep crying glory it's because each time they go around more revelation of God is revealed and they can't keep from crying glory. The newness in more revelation creates excitement. This builds you up and in turn builds the church.

No matter what place you are in God, you should be desirous of knowing something new; new in the Spirit and new in the Word. This will always give you more life and strength in your natural and spiritual life. It gives the unbelieving world evidence of God's presence in your life. This evidence can be expressed in so many different ways, but it speaks of changes and newness which could only have been caused by someone other than your self, JESUS. Remember (Psalm 36:10) "And in your light we see light."

EXALTING HIM

"Therefore whoever confesses Me before men, him I will also confess before my Father who is in heaven." (Mt. 10:32) Sometimes we think exalting and praising God on a one-on-one relationship is all that is needed to please Him. Wrong! When you glorify Jesus before people you are exalting Him; and He requires this. All of Psalm 145 describes praising Him both ways. The first three verses speak of praising Him from your heart. "I will extol You...I will bless Your name forever and ever." (:1) "Every day will I bless You and I will praise Your name forever and ever." (:2) "Great is the Lord and greatly to be praised; And His greatness is unsearchable." (:3) Then in verse (:4) it says, "One generation shall praise Your works to another and shall declare Your mighty acts." Also in (:5) "I will meditate on the glorious splendor of Your majesty, And on Your wondrous works." It is extremely important for parents to teach their children the ways of the Lord. Joshua's generation failed to do that. (Judges 2:10,11) states, "... another generation arose after them who did not know the Lord, nor the work which He had done for Israel. Then the children of Israel did evil..." "They forsook the Lord." (:13) "And the anger of the Lord was hot against Israel. So He delivered them into the hands of plunderers who despoiled them; and He sold them into the hands of their enemies..." (:14) The penalty for the sins of the fathers for failing to teach their children came upon their children and further generations. There is a price to pay for not staying consistent with God and speaking of Him and what He has done for you. (:6,7) Likewise, the more you speak of His blessings and favor in your life, the more your life and the life of your children will be blessed and favored. "Men shall speak of the might of Your awesome acts, And I will declare Your greatness. They shall utter the memory of Your great goodness, And shall sing of Your righteousness." (Psalm 145:6,7) David reiterates God's goodness in (:8, 9), "The Lord is gracious, and full of compassion, slow to anger, and great in mercy. The Lord is good to all, And his tender mercies are over all His works." With all the negativity in the world, let us devote ourselves to speaking of God's goodness as David did. (:10-12) "All Your works shall praise You, (are not we also His works?), O Lord, and Your saints shall bless You. They shall speak of the glory of Your kingdom, And talk of Your power, To make known to the sons of men His mighty acts, And the glorious majesty of His kingdom." God knows it when you speak of Him in public. The more you do this, the more doors He will open for you to do it. Then you will have even more exciting things to talk about as you see Him watch over His Word to perform it!

LOVE PERFECTS LOVE

"No one has seen God at any time. If we love one another, God abides in us, and His love has been perfected in us." (1 Jn. 4:12) God is love! (:8) God doesn't want to stay in places where there isn't love. Pretense, lip-service to God and others, self-righteous behavior all done under the banner of Christianity is sin. There is no faith involved in any of that. In the Old Testament, staying right with God required sacrifice. It still does, but of a different kind. Now, are we willing to sacrifice our time to praise and worship God; to deny ourselves enough to be a fool for Jesus in witnessing to the unsaved; to lighten your neighbor's burden? This is the real kind of Christian love. Jesus gave up the freedom of heaven, became enslaved to a body of human flesh, and suffered everything a human could suffer including death. There is no sacrifice we could ever make that could ever come close to that sacrifice. The love of God is based on sacrifice. When we say we love someone have we sacrificed anything for that person? This is the kind of love that speaks the loudest.

Your life of faith will not grow unless your love grows with it. "For in Christ Jesus neither circumcision nor uncircumcision avails anything, but faith working through love." (Gal. 5:6) How often do we forget that and get caught up in works with no anointing? Paul commended the Thessalonians in his second letter to them when he wrote, "We are bound to give thank God always for you, brethren, as it is fitting, because your faith grows exceedingly, and the love of every one of you all abounds toward each other." (2 Thess. 1:3) I believe when Paul wrote this in his second letter, he remembered what he wrote them in his first letter when he said he was praying for them to, "...perfect what is lacking in your faith," (1Thess.3:10) and in (:12), "And may the Lord make you increase and abound in love to one another and to all, just as we do to you." I believe his prayer was answered. Faith and love can't be disconnected.

Do weightlifters use strength to become stronger? Don't you become happier when you give happiness to others? This is how love grows. If we live a life which represents love we are living continually in God's favor, God's strength, God's anointing, and God's pleasure. If things do not seem to be working, advancing, growing, prospering, or getting blessed check your love life. I believe it is there you will find your answer. By letting the love of God be poured out from your heart by the Holy Spirit you will be a blessing and be blessed. (Rom.5:5)

WIND AND SPIRIT

The Holy Spirit is described as a wind. On the day of Pentecost, "And suddenly there came a sound from heaven, as of a rushing mighty wind and it filled the whole house where they were sitting." (Acts 2:2) In (Jn. 3:8) it says whoever is born of the Spirit hears the sound of the wind, (Holy Spirit). In both cases the Holy Spirit is speaking. That is why we must be born of the Holy Spirit to understand the move (sound) of the Holy Spirit. The Holy Spirit is always speaking. That is why we must be led by the Holy Spirit to do the work of God. There is no growth, no fruit, if the church world is led by the 'sounds' of religion, theology, or anything self-centered. "As you do not know what is the way of the wind.......So you do not know the works of God who makes everything." (Eccles.11:5)

The world is full of sounds; both good and bad. Whatever is said contributes to either a good spiritual wind or a bad spiritual wind. When Bildad rebukes Job in (Job 8:2) he said, "How long will you speak these things, And the words of your mouth be like a strong wind." In places where bad words and bad events happen you can feel a bad spiritual wind. A person with unbelief and doubt wavers. That person is described as one who, "is like a wave of the sea driven and tossed by the wind." (James 1:6) The opposite is also true. People are attracted to places and people who say and do strong, encouraging, and uplifting things. "The words of a man's mouth are deep waters; The wellspring of wisdom is a flowing brook." (Prov.18:4) You create your own atmosphere by the words you speak and the sounds you allow into it.

Bad doctrines create very bad winds. The Bible warns, "that we should no longer be children, tossed to and fro and carried about with every wind of doctrine, by the trickery of men...." (Eph. 4:14) The church and political world are loaded with these bad winds to the point laws are being passed to eliminate true Christian teaching. Just as Jesus rebuked the wind (bad wind) in (Lk. 8:24) it is up to the true church to rebuke the bad winds of doctrine, religion, carnality and anything which opposes itself against the knowledge of God. God wants to raise up an end time army. It is an army which will prophecy to the wind and speak life into all the dry bones of the church all around them. It is a sound from the Holy Spirit through the church which will breathe life into the unsaved and revival to the church. A new definition of being filled with the Holy Spirit will be realized as we carry the wind of the Holy Spirit with us.

ARISE

"Arise, shine; For your light has come! And the glory of the Lord is risen upon you." (Isa.60:1) The majority of the church world is still asleep and needs to rise up and be who God has called them to be. It must be understood and acknowledged that the church world has lived so far below par for so long it has associated its' position of being below par as normal. As God's Spirit is being released in new dimensions and power, God wants His church to be able to respond to Him at that level and produce fruit at that level. Few Christians are able to. Why? Hosea said, "<u>My people</u> are destroyed for lack of knowledge. Because you have rejected knowledge I also will reject you from being priest for Me." (Hos.4:6) Jesus also said, "Every branch <u>in Me</u> that does not bear fruit He takes away…" (Jn.15:2) God is addressing His own people, not the unsaved in the world. The church world is so accustomed to receiving teaching on a level they are comfortable with, new revelations of who they can be and what they can really do in Jesus are rejected. That's why it is often difficult to tell the difference between people in the church and those in the world. That's why there is just as much sin in the church. Christians do not want to rise up out of the same mind set which was on the Laodicean church. When they thought they had everything God said they had nothing and called them to repent. (Rev.3:14-22) The same is true today.

What becomes a living reality to you as a Christian is something which is received by revelation; not just the word which is preached or taught. "But God has revealed them to us through His Spirit. For the Spirit searches all things, yes, the deep things of God." (1 Cor.2:10) Have you ever dialed a wrong telephone number and got the information you needed? It is time for all true Christians to rise up in Jesus name and expect God to do new exciting things in and through them. It is time to become a General in God's army, not a Private. "For in Him dwells all the fullness of the Godhead bodily and you are complete in Him who is the head of all principality and power." (Col.2:9,10) It is time for Christians to see themselves as so complete in Jesus, they can see a tremendous amount of souls saved and healed through them. If the glory of the latter house (church) is supposed to be greater than that of the former (Haggai 2:9) and the present day church has not even come close to operating at the level of the former house (early church) something is wrong. It is time for Christians to see themselves as having power over all power of the devil (Lk.10:19) and then acting like it without compromise to God's word or principles. It is time to possess the land. God is giving more strength than ever in the Holy Spirit to do it!

IN HIM

There is an earnest desire among Christians to be used by God. There is a growth process of going from milk to meat; from babyhood to maturity; and from knowledge to power. This process takes longer for some, and shorter for others. During this process one most important revelation must be received before any Christian is effective for Jesus on any level. This revelation is anything done in the name of Jesus must be done in and through Him. A Christian can live their whole life and see absolutely nothing happen. The name of Jesus and the word of God can be used with no results because it is spoken from a soulish realm with no anointing.

Do you want to be effective and have fruit dripping off you everywhere you go? You can be there. I didn't say get there. Get there implies works. Works imply self. First consider Peter, John and Paul. When Peter walked down the street people were healed in his shadow. (Acts 5:15) He didn't wait for a 'special anointing'. When Dorcas died they called for him to come and raise her from the dead. He did. (Acts 9:36-41) All Peter and John had to say at the gate beautiful was, "what I do have I give you, In the name of Jesus Christ of Nazareth rise up and walk," and the lame man was healed. (Acts 3:6) When Paul was bitten by a viper, he didn't wait for a 'special anointing' to shake it off. (Acts 28:5) Run-of-the-mill Pentecostal churches don't even know about this place in the Holy Spirit Peter, John, and Paul were in. Some denominational churches are clueless. It is a place of being totally absorbed in the person of Jesus. Then you give of Him, Jesus, so easily, supernatural signs and wonders are always following you. So, how do you realize, "in Him we live and move and have our being?" (Acts 17:28) First of all you have to realize you don't represent yourself or even care about representing yourself in any way. If you do certain percentages of the soulish realm creep into things which can only be accomplished by the work of the Holy Spirit and things are hindered or stopped depending on the percentages. Before you try to minister anything to anybody say to yourself and God that you disassociate yourself from everything regarding self. Acknowledge you don't represent yourself in any single way. Disengage all soulish thinking and be still inside yourself. (Psm.46:10) Then step up to the plate and speak with His authority as His ambassador fully representing Him. (2 Cor.5:20) Then God watches over His word to perform it. (Rom.4:21) You don't.

The growth process is necessary. The twelve disciples were with Jesus for three years before they received the Holy Spirit and were sent. Maybe Peter, John and Paul had a deeper revelation of being totally absorbed in Jesus. Perhaps more would have been written about and from the other disciples if they had the same depth. Maybe if you understand this message you can understand why Paul had to consider himself dead to do the things he did for Jesus. (Gal.2:20) The church world in general is living far below its' potential. I dare say if all true Christians received and lived out this one revelation there would be such a change whole communities and cities would be saved. The church is called to change the culture surrounding it. Unfortunately, the culture has changed the church into something way too liberal, weak and self-centered. However, God is now speaking to the church world with an urgency in no uncertain terms to change. There will be those who will walk in the light of this revelation and stand out in their community like true beacons of His light. There will be those who won't. God is calling His people to work with

Him in new and powerful ways to see more people saved and healed than ever before. It is my prayer for every Christian to rise up into this new intimacy with our Savior; that all parts of self are lost in the shuffle, and the fullness of God to the greatest extent possible is shown/shone through us.

COMPASSION

"And when Jesus went out, He saw a great multitude, and He <u>was moved with compassion for them</u>, and healed their sick." (Mt.14:14) "And Jesus, when he came out, saw a great multitude, and <u>was moved with compassion for them</u> because they were like sheep not having a shepherd. So He began to teach them many things." (Mk.6:34) In one instance he healed them; in another he taught them. Jesus didn't just have compassion. He was moved with compassion toward the people. Action always followed his compassion. The same should be true for Christians. Prayer alone shouldn't be substituted for good works. Having compassion without works is like having faith without works. It's dead. (James 2:17)

The words 'compassion for', or in some translations 'compassion toward', or 'compassion on' mean Jesus literally suffered in pain with the same afflictions the people had. It was far beyond having pity. He felt their suffering to the extent he had to do something about it. The apostle, John, wrote, "And there are also many other things that Jesus did, which, if they were written one by one, I suppose that even the world itself could not contain the books that would be written." (Jn.21:25)

Sometimes we overlook doing just a little thing for someone that would have made a huge difference in their day and or life. At times there is a tendency to look or wait for an anointing you already have. By that, I mean if you know Jesus has called you to do something and are led by the Holy Spirit you already have the anointing to do it. You don't need any extra confirmations or goose-bumps. The works Jesus calls us to do are already planned and complete in His mind. (Eph.2:10) All we have to do is obey His calling. Many times there is a natural human tendency to stop, analyze, and evaluate every situation once you hear from God. This gives the devil plenty of opportunities to put enough fear and doubt into our thinking to stop us from acting in faith alone. But, the Bible tells us, "the just shall live by faith." (Gal.3:11) This pure walk in faith alone truly understands God's ways are not man's ways. Faith alone will act on God's word and direction without question. Faith alone will act on the small things and the big things on a daily and long term basis. All God is looking for is someone who makes him or herself available to be used by Him. Just ask God to use you with whatever natural or spiritual gifts you have. He will work you into His schedule of daily events in one way or another, whether or not it is a prayer, a gift, or a good work. If you make a difference in someone's life, you will see a difference made in them. Let the name of Jesus be glorified in everything you do!

MORE COMPASSION

"You must be compassionate, as your Father also is compassionate." (Lk.6:36 kjv) Jesus set an example of compassion for His disciples. When Jesus took His disciples across the Sea of Galilee to Gadara they encountered a great storm which Jesus had to stop. His disciples feared for their lives. Little did they know He was taking them on this trip for one reason. When they got to Gadara, ".....immediately there met him out of the tombs, a man with an unclean spirit." (Mk.5:2) This man came to Jesus with four or six thousand (a legion) devils in him, but he came to Jesus; and Jesus dealt with him just like he was. What is our excuse not to come to Jesus before or after salvation with our situations? The compassion of Jesus receives anyone who will come to Him. Are you any worse than this demoniac? I don't think so. Jesus took this man and delivered him to complete mental and physical health. When the townspeople saw what Jesus had done they told Him to leave their coasts. (:17) When the man who was healed requested to go with Jesus it was not permitted, but Jesus said, "Go home to your friends and tell them what great things the Lord has done for you, and how He has had compassion on you." (:19) Then Jesus left with His disciples and sailed back to the other side of the sea. So, Jesus had taken His disciples on an arduous sailing trip across a sea and back for them to witness this one act of compassion on a demonized man. He probably amazed His disciples with this kind of love. In the end, the whole city of Decapolis heard about Jesus through this healed man. Nothing is recorded about how His disciples responded, but I'm sure Jesus did this to impress them about what He was willing to do to touch one very rejected and hurting person.

It is also recorded His disciples, "marveled that He talked with a woman," (Jn.4:27). This was the Samaritan woman at the well who was a loose living Gentile. He had already told His disciples He did not come to condemn the world, but that the world through Him might be saved. (Jn.3:17) His disciples didn't get the message immediately. When James and John wanted to call down fire on a Samaritan village which would not receive them Jesus rebuked them and told them they didn't know what spirit they were of. (Lk.9:52-56) He explicitly told them He did not come to destroy men's lives but to save them. Because of His ministry to the Samaritan woman, many salvations happened in her city of Sychar. Because Jesus showed compassion on people who were normally rejected by society whole cities heard about Jesus. That kind of compassion gets that kind of results.

OUR GREAT FUTURE

"Having made known to us the mystery of His will, according to His good pleasure which He purposed in Himself, that in the dispensation of the fullness of the times He might gather together in one all things in Christ, both which are in heaven, and which are on earth, in Him. In Him also we have obtained an inheritance, being predestinated according to the purpose of Him who works all things according to the counsel of His will, that we, who first trusted in Christ should be to the praise of His glory. In Him you also trusted after you heard the word of truth, the gospel of your salvation; in whom also having believed, you were sealed with the Holy Spirit of promise, Who is the guarantee of our inheritance until the redemption of the purchased possession to the praise of His glory." (Eph.1:9-14)

The universal questions of, 'why was I born?', and, 'why do I exist?' are found in these scriptures. Our God of goodness has revealed to the early apostles and therefore to us His secret plans for mankind. *Everything for eternity will be in Jesus Christ!* That has, is, and will always be God's plan. It will happen for all of our eternity, for all who have made Jesus their Lord in this lifetime. God has planned we inherit the riches of heaven through Jesus. He has given us the Holy Spirit to remind us of our wonderful eternity. We have the proof of our great inheritance with us all the time. We have the answer to anyone who would ask why we are so secure in our future by having such a personal relationship with Jesus. The inner witness of His presence gives us so much confidence, that words and ministry come easy. God wants us to have a very rich and enjoyable friendship with Jesus now, so the world can be convinced of how happy our life will be for eternity. It's all about sharing a tremendous relationship with a God of love now and forever. That's Christianity!

Things of the Holy Spirit are not understood by the natural mind. That's why we as Christians must make known by the way we live, the work of the Holy Spirit in us. That is the evidence, the proof, the promise, of our life in Jesus now and forever. These six scriptures in Ephesians are enough to explain to anyone why they need Jesus. It is so simple to understand God's ultimate plan for mankind. He created us to be with Him! He loves us. He has always loved us. He has given mankind the opportunity to return to Him and enjoy His riches for all of eternity through Jesus. Why would we want to explain our God being any other way? Lead people to Jesus. They will never regret it for all of eternity!

REWARDS

We could never give back to Jesus as much as He has given to us; His life in exchange for our eternity with Him instead of spending it in hell. That one fact alone, the reward of heaven should be enough to make us want to serve Him with gladness all the days of our lives. But God in his mercies and love even rewards us in this lifetime for our service to Him. "And every one who has left houses, or brothers or sisters, or father or mother, or wife, or children, or lands for My name's sake, shall receive a hundredfold, and inherit eternal life." (Mt. 19:29) Any sacrifice you make toward establishing the Kingdom of God will have temporal and eternal rewards one hundred times your sacrifice.

If you live your life for the purpose of being successful oftentimes you will not make it. There is much frustration and turmoil in living only for temporal rewards that only satisfy your self. But when you live your life for the purpose of being a blessing to someone else then success will come. Jesus warned of making a show of your 'holiness' or giving. He said there would be no reward in that. However, if you do three things in secret, giving, praying, and fasting, God will reward you openly. (Mt. Chap. 6) When we set our affection on heavenly rewards our daily life is filled with many fine choices. Rewards in heaven are according to the works of the believer. "Now he who plants and he who waters are one, and each one will receive his own reward according to his own labor." (1 Cor.3:8) Our labor must be based on the foundation of Jesus Christ. (:11) It is only this work which shall last when tried by fire, and only this work shall receive a reward. (:14) It is God who builds His church. Therefore whatever we do we must do with Him. "For we are God's fellow workers…" (:9) When you build with eternal materials you have eternal rewards.

A believer is rewarded with the crown of life for faithfulness and endurance. "Blessed is the man who endures temptation; for when he has been approved, he will receive the crown of life which the Lord has promised to those who love him." (James 1:12) Jesus said, "For whoever desires to save his life will lose it, but whoever loses his life for My sake and the gospel's, will save it." (Mk.8:35) When you lose your life for the sake of the gospel Jesus will let you know what He wants you to do. Then as you live your life in obedience to His call on your life, He is working with you. Your works will be based on Him, not yourself. You will be more concerned about eternal rewards and get them. But also remember (Mt.6:33), "But seek first the kingdom of God and His righteousness and all these things shall be added to you."

SECRET OF FAITH

"Therefore, I say to you, whatever things you ask when you pray, believe that you receive them and you <u>will</u> have them." (Mk.11:24) It is imperative your faith must work by love, (Gal.5:6); you must live with a forgiving heart; (Mk.11:25, 26) and you must have any sin confessed and repented of (Psm.32:5). That is a given. However, there is a principle of faith, when adhered to, will birth your miracle. First of all, it is right to expect the healing, or deliverance or miracle to be manifested when you minister. Jesus didn't have to wait. We should expect the same. However, I guess if the answers to all our prayers were answered instantly we wouldn't need much faith, and we would become a bunch of mechanical, robotic saints. So, timing is an integral part of God's plans for eternity and for individuals. This is how our faith in Jesus, not self, is tested.

So, what is the secret to making faith work besides the givens? Consider the birth of Jesus. His birth was not a miracle. <u>The miracle happened when He was conceived by the Holy Spirit. Then, when He was born the miracle was birthed</u>. That is the secret of faith working. It doesn't matter what the need is. If you can believe when you pray that the answer is conceived/received in your spirit you will carry your answers to prayer with you all the time. That will give you a positive overcoming attitude regardless of the circumstances. You will not bow down to circumstances and feel hopeless at all. Your faith will be constantly at work in your heart. You will smile with the peace of God and point your finger at the storm and rebuke it. Your trust is in the God you belong to. Your attitude is a carryover of the Holy Spirit working. Out of weakness you will be made strong. (Heb.11:34) You will stand on the truth and not believe the devil's lies about living with false humility and weakness in order to 'please' God. NO! If your life is a shining example of God's favor and blessing you are showing the world the outcome of your faith and the change which has been made inside you regardless of circumstance. God wants you to believe you can reign as a king in this lifetime. Doesn't the Bible say Jesus has made us kings and priests to God? (Rev.1:6) If the Bible says the truth has set you free, (Jn.8:32) you can take your answers right off God's pages, put them in your heart, draw life every day from them and live in the overcoming, victory already provided by Jesus! Do you dare to believe God for everything good in your life? When you dedicate your life to serving God and others success will come. God will make answers to prayer happen quickly, so He can elevate you to the next level of use for His glory. Serve God and others with all your heart and God will go beyond meeting your needs. Your own personal life will shine brighter than ever before!

LIFE

The real definition of life is being with God. When a person can understand what life is from this perspective it changes everything in their life. For an unbeliever it brings the need to be saved into a clearer focus. For a believer it puts a deeper desire in their heart to know Jesus and comprehend what He has really done for them. The believer now is ministering life itself to people who want eternal life, and using the God-given tools to help people live a happy, healthy, secure, natural life. With this definition of life we can ask ourselves if what we are saying and doing leads to being or not being with God; enjoying life or not enjoying life in every situation.

Life with God must not remain in infancy. Our spiritual life grows from milk to meat just like our natural life grows. "But strong meat belongs to them that are of full age even those who by reason of use have their senses exercised to discern between both good and evil." (Heb.5:14 kjv) God wants us to grow into adulthood with Him. John writes, "I write to you, fathers, because you have known Him who is from the beginning..." (1 Jn.2:13) It is being with someone you know that will give you the same character and abilities of that person. Such is our relationship with Jesus as we are changed from glory to glory into His image. That's why we must dedicate our lives to knowing Him.

Most people spend so much time concentrating on what serves their natural life they miss out on what real life is. Jesus calls himself life in (Jn.14:6) "I am the way the truth and the life..." God calls Himself life in (Psm.36:9) "For with You is the fountain of life; In your light we see light." The Holy Spirit is called life. Ezekiel said in (37:14) "I will put my Spirit in you and you shall live..." Everything about the Father, Son, and Holy Spirit is life!

Now as this truth is applied and worked out in our lives we will be speaking life and everything which represents life to each other. We will put aside the issues which cause divisions and in the eyes of eternity are trite and meaningless. Our words will be the words of life. Are we contributing to someone's happiness and well-being by what we say and do? "If anyone speaks, let him speak as the oracles of God.....that in all things God may be glorified through Jesus Christ to whom belong the glory and the dominion forever and ever. Amen." (1 Pet.4:11) As we minister life to others by speaking God's words with God's love the same will be ministered to us. As God is the fountain of life, and we let more and more of that fountain fill us, we become a fountain of life to others. In our light they will see light and others will soon see light in them and others will see light in them..... Let our lives be a fountain of life.

THE BUS DRIVER

The bus driver said, "Every day I see people get in and out of this bus. Some of them glance at me; some of them wave at me; some of them go right by without even looking. It is very sad because none of them know me. Some of them do not want to know me at all. They are going along for the ride, looking nice and pretty, but not knowing who is carrying them. If they really knew where this bus could take them, all of them would want to know me. If they really knew the beautiful places I could take them, and the beautiful journey they could have with me everyone would want to sit in the front seat. I would also introduce everyone to each other and they would all know each other in a very special way by knowing me. My heart grieves because my friendship and my love for them is so real and will last forever. Even though this ride with me may have a few bumps and a few detours from time to time they all can be safe with me. I'm not afraid to take them through all kinds of weather in any season because my hand is always on the wheel. I love my passengers and I regret seeing them leave my bus, not knowing if they will ever come back and ride with me again. I want to talk with every one of them, so they can really know me and know what a great driver I am. I always wait at each bus stop until everyone gets on even if they are late. I don't want them to get on any other bus or ride with any other driver. I will drive this bus forever and carry anyone, hoping someday they will strike up a conversation and really get to know me and my love for them."

So it is with people who go to church, but don't know Jesus. He's waiting.

LaVergne, TN USA
17 March 2010
176276LV00002B/104/A